THE PAIN THAT NEVER LEFT ME

BY BABITA THAKUR

BlueRose ONE.com
Stories Matter
NewDelhi • London

BLUEROSE PUBLISHERS
India | U.K.

BlueRose ONE
Stories Matter
NewDelhi • London

For permissions requests or inquiries regarding this publication, please contact:

BLUEROSE PUBLISHERS
www.BlueRoseONE.com
info@bluerosepublishers.com
+91 8882 898 898
+4407342408967

ISBN: 978-93-7542-798-8

First Edition: March 2026

Echoes of My Father's Silence

Some wounds are not visible.

Some grief never ends.

Some love refuses to let go — even when life does.

And some moments don't just hurt… they echo forever.

When a sudden medical emergency shatters the fragile rhythm of ordinary life, one daughter is thrust into a world ruled by fear, uncertainty, and silent prayers whispered in hospital corridors. Time slows into unbearable stillness. Breath feels heavy. Every second stretches into an eternity where hope trembles between life and loss.

Machines hum where voices once laughed.

Eyes search for answers no one can give.

And the heart learns what it means to break… quietly… repeatedly… without warning.

Strength is tested in ways the soul never prepares for — in sleepless nights, in trembling hands that refuse to give up, in the crushing helplessness of loving someone you cannot save from suffering.

In this deeply moving and emotionally unfiltered memoir, moments of helplessness collide with fierce, unyielding love, and the quiet resilience of the human spirit emerges through unimaginable pain. Every page carries the weight of reality — the unbearable waiting, the fragile flicker of hope, the deafening silence of uncertainty, and the haunting truth that some experiences do not simply pass through us…

They remake us.

They mark us.

They stay.

This is not just a story of illness.

It is a story of love that refuses to break.

Of courage that rises even while collapsing within.

Of grief that settles deep into the bones.

Of memories that breathe long after voices fall silent.

It is about the moment you realise life will never return to what it once was — and the quiet, devastating acceptance that follows.

Raw, intimate, and profoundly human, this unforgettable book does not simply tell a story — it places you inside it. You will feel the waiting. You will feel the fear. You will feel the love that refuses to loosen its grip… even when everything else slips away.

And long after the final page is turned, when the world grows quiet again, something will remain with you.

Because some pain does not fade.

Some love does not end.

Some memories never loosen their hold.

Some pain does not pass.

It lives within you.

Contents

CHAPTER 1

The Call That Changed Everything

It was 6:00 AM.

The sky outside my window remained half-asleep—washed in pale blue, streaked with grey like faint brushstrokes across the horizon. No sounds of brooms sweeping the lanes, no footsteps, no morning prayers. There was a mosque nearby, but no azan to break the silence. It felt as if the world had paused—too still for an April morning.

I sat at my study table, cradling a warm mug of tea between my palms. The steam curled slowly into the cold air, vanishing before my eyes. I brought it close to my face, hoping the warmth would steady me. It should've been a normal day—quiet, slow, peaceful.

But something was wrong.

A strange heaviness settled on my chest, as though something dark and uncertain had begun to stir. I glanced outside again. The silence seemed suffocating, weighed down by its own ominous presence. A deep sense of foreboding gnawed at me.

Then—

RINGGGG.

The phone rang, sharp and sudden, slicing through the stillness like a scream. My eyes widened in alarm. My mother never called this early—she knew I was usually getting ready for work.

Her name flashed on the screen, and an instant wave of dread hit me. My hands turned cold. My mind whispered: Something's wrong.

I answered.

"M-m-m… your father…" Her voice was barely there—quivering, broken.

"Maa? What happened?" I asked, my throat tightening.

"Something's happened to your father…" she sobbed, struggling to speak.

Her voice was filled with panic—raw, unfiltered fear I had never heard before.

"He's not speaking… he can't stand," she said, gasping, her words disjointed, tumbling out in desperate pieces.

My chest clenched. My vision blurred. I gripped the edge of the table to keep from collapsing.

"What do you mean he can't stand? Please explain properly!" My voice trembled, desperate for clarity amid the nightmare unfolding over the phone.

"I don't know… I can't figure it out… He fainted suddenly, then vomited… His face was flickering… And then… he just collapsed…" Her voice broke into a sob.

I began pacing the room, my tea untouched, now cold. My hands trembled as I unlocked my phone and searched for the my symptoms she described.

Stroke. Paralysis. Emergency.

The words flashed before me like warning sirens. My stomach twisted into knots.

"Maa, is anyone there with you?" I asked, trying to hold my voice steady, though fear engulfed me.

"I called Sahil and his mother, the neighbors… They're coming. We're taking him to the hospital," she said, trembling with each word.

"Okay… okay… listen to me…" But I had no words left. I felt helpless—like screaming underwater. I wanted to be there, to teleport through the phone, to shatter the walls and hold the situation together.

Somewhere deep inside, a voice whispered: You always knew a day like this would come. You just didn't know it would feel this way.

"He got up normally… He vomited… Then his body froze. One side stiffened. Now he's lying there, not saying anything," she continued.

Cold sweat formed on my forehead. I looked out the window again. The sky hadn't brightened much. The air was heavier now, as though the day itself held its breath.

I called my sister, Disha didi. No answer.

Tried again. Nothing.

She always sleep late. I cursed under my breath and called my mother again.

"Maa, are you ready to leave for the hospital?" I asked.

"No… I can't find his medical reports," she sobbed. "He mentioned Aaman Hospital, but I don't know where the previous reports of his medical history are…"

I could hear hurried footsteps, the shuffling of bags, Sahil's voice giving instructions. Chaos unfolding.

I imagined my father—struggling to speak through slurred words, aware yet trapped in his body.

The clock showed 6:57 AM.

The strange stillness of the morning had morphed into a storm of fear and confusion. My body tensed. My face shivered.

And deep in my bones, I knew—

Nothing would ever be the same again.

It was the 1st of April. A mild winter still clung to the air. I sat in my work station chair, unable to do anything but call my mother again and again to get update of each second.

"Why haven't you left yet? What's going on?" My voice trembled, my skin pale, my heart heavy with dread.

"I can't find his medical reports," she repeated again same desperate. "I've searched everywhere—drawers, shelves… nothing."

The house must have been in utter chaos. Papers scattered. Memories torn apart.

I thought of Papa. What had happened to him so suddenly? I had spoken to him last night—he was perfectly fine.

Meanwhile, Sahil helped Papa into fresh clothes. His body was limp, his eyes cloudy.

It was nearly 7:00 AM when Papa whispered, barely audible, "Get the medical reports from Aaman Hospital…"

By 7:30, the taxi finally arrived.

I called my brother.

"You know something's happened to Papa?" I asked, my throat tight with panic.

I called my sister again—shivering, desperate, praying she would answer. Still nothing.

Then I called my brother-in-law, Jiju.

"Hello?" he answered.

"Something's happened to Papa. One side of his body is stiff… He vomited…"

"What?!"

"Please… please help them."

"He : Ask them to leave for the city hospital. I'll be there in half an hour."

Time passed, but Papa still hadn't reached the hospital. Each second a stab of helplessness.

I called my mother again.

"Why the delay? Are you still at home?" I tried to sound calm, though I was far from it.

"I can't find anything," she said, voice trembling. "I don't know where he kept his documents. Please… I'm trying."

Finally, my sister called back.

"Kya hua? In hindi (what happened??)"

"Papa's one side is stiff… He vomited… I don't know what's happening."

It was now 8:00 AM. Every second stabbed me harder.

My subconscious screamed: The storm is coming.

"Have you left yet?" I asked to mom again.

"Just locking the house," my mother replied.

At last, they left for the hospital.

But this was only the beginning.

I was terrified. My chest ached. My stomach is hollow. No part of me could accept this. Fathers are fortresses. We grow up believing they can never break, never fall.

But now...

They arrived at the City Government Hospital. From the symptoms I'd Googled, I knew—it wasn't mild or temporary. This was serious. Deadly serious.

My mother stood in shock, lost, surrounded by people yet utterly alone.

I wanted to scream. To shatter the distance. To be there. But I was helpless.

"Where is he now? Has the doctor seen him?" I asked.

"I don't know… they took him somewhere…" Her voice cracked.

"Somewhere? Where, Maa? Can you ask someone?"

"I'm alone… I don't understand anything…"

Her dependency on Papa made her unable to hold up in this panic.

"Don't worry," I said, "I'm flying home today itself. It's only three hours from Bangalore. You're not alone."

But I didn't believe it myself.

Soon, Disha didi and Jiju reached the hospital. I called my brother Lakshay

"Papa is very critical."

"What happened?"

"He's at the City Government Hospital. Maa didn't want to tell you, but I had to."

"…Okay," he replied, and hung up.

Around 10 AM, my phone rang again.

"Papa's had half of his body gone dead," Disha didi said.

"What?!" My heart stopped. A fear so huge it drowned me. My ears seemed to block out sound tooooonnnnn!!!

"We got a brain CT scan done. The doctor referred him to Chandigarh Hospital."

The world went silent.

My breath caught. I was frozen. Everything blurred.

Was this a dream?

No. This was real.

"We're taking him to Chandigarh," Disha didi said. She hadn't told Mom yet—her voice cracked, speechless with fear.

"Please… go fast. As fast as you can," I whispered.

"What about Mom? Who will go with her?"

"I'll go," Disha didi said.

I hung up and called my office. Took a off from work. My manager seems supportive so he approved easily.

I tried to book a flight to Chandigarh, but my hands trembled, my eyes burned. I couldn't think. Couldn't breathe.

Meanwhile, they arranged an ambulance.

They were on their way.

the invisible storm had arrived in our life.

CHAPTER 2

My Helpless Panic

As the ambulance sped toward Chandigarh, I remained glued to my phone, my fingers trembling uncontrollably as I kept calling them.

"Maa… Disha didi… Prem bhaiya one of my relative… Where are you now? Have you reached yet?"

Each ring seemed to stretch longer, each unanswered call tightening the knot of fear in my chest.

At the same time, I was desperately trying to book a flight to Chandigarh.

My hands shook so badly that I couldn't even type properly. My fingers pressed the keys at random, each attempt failing, the screen freezing, the website loading too slowly.

The whole process felt like wading through thick fog.

I opened the airline's website again and again—searching for flights, trying to hold myself together.

One… two… three attempts.

Nothing.

"No… no…" I whispered, my voice cracking, eyes burning with unshed tears.

Each second was a battle against time itself.

I searched for flight timings—

Airlines… No available flights in the next few hours.

My body was numb, my breath shallow.

My fingers, weak and trembling, barely responded.

I tried again—

Finally, a glimmer of hope—a flight departing at mid night to chandigarh .

But the process felt impossible. My mind was scattered. My heart pounding too fast, my vision blurred.

Could I really manage to complete this?

I forced myself to focus.

I filled in the details, the card numbers, the passenger information…

One click.

Confirmation.

The ticket was booked

But the sense of relief was fleeting, swallowed immediately by the gnawing guilt and fear.

Because at that moment, none of it felt real.

The ticking clock, the distance stretching further, the hopeless weight of helplessness—

They were all too much to bear.

My mind screamed: Hurry… Hurry… Don't let him slip away…

But I knew… time was no longer on our side.

CHAPTER 3

The Journey Begins

It was 2:00 PM.

The ambulance had finally arrived at Aaman Hospital.

I called again.

Me: "Reached?"

Sister exhaled loudly, a sound heavy with relief.

She: "Yes… we've reached."

I let out a shaky breath, trying to steady myself. For a fleeting moment, a tiny flicker of hope surfaced—perhaps we had arrived at a safe zone. Maybe this was the beginning of something positive.

But I didn't know then…

This wasn't even the trailer.

I hung up.

At that moment, I stood by my suitcase, fingers paused mid-air.

It's just for 2–3 days, I told myself.

Why was I packing so much? Should I take my office laptop? A small bag should be enough.

For a brief second, normalcy peeked through the haze—as if I were still part of the world where preparing for short trips was routine.

I called sister again.

Me: "Hello? How's the situation now? Have they started treatment?"

Sister: "No… there's no doctor yet."

Me: "What?! It's a brain haemorrhage… how is there no doctor?"

She "It's a small hospital…"

Me: "Then why did you come here?"

She: "Mummy said Aaman Hospital. Papa has suggested this in morning …"

My heart sank deeper.

Me: "I'll be reaching by midnight. I have booked my flight. How many days will it take to recover him? And… how will I come alone from the airport to the hospital in the middle of the night?"

I spoke gently, trying to sound composed.

She: "We'll figure it out. But… come prepared. You might have to stay at the hospital for several days now."

Her words hit me like a sudden blow.

Until now, I'd been fooling myself into believing this would pass quickly.

I hadn't packed properly. I hadn't eaten. My hands were cold, my face damp with tears I hadn't noticed falling.

Everything inside me was fracturing—hollow, numb. My chest ached, as though something was clawing from within.

It was 3:00 PM.

Me: “Any update? Has the doctor arrived?”

Sister: “Yes… they’ve taken him inside. He’ll be shifted to ICU soon.”

A fragile wave of relief washed over me. Something… anything to cling to.

I ordered food—idli. I hadn’t eaten all day. But hunger didn’t register. I was simply trying to remember how to function.

Then the phone rang.

Lakshay :“I’m coming with you.”

Me: “Okay… I’ll send you the flight details. Book it now.”

Lakshay: "Done.”

Call ended.

I sat in my room, surrounded by half-packed bags and scattered clothes, my mind far away—in the hospital corridors, the beeping machines, the whispers of doctors.

I was preparing to travel…

Unaware that I was actually preparing to step into an ocean of sorrows.

My hands trembled. The untouched idli grew cold in my palm. I couldn’t eat. My throat tightened. The air around me felt strange—hot, dry, suffocating. Every breath weighed heavy, even the wind.

I decided to take the bus instead of a taxi. A nightmare from a few days ago—a reckless, unsafe ride—still haunted me. My instincts screamed: Avoid that risk again.

Incident brief: In March month

I had been seeing my father in my dreams, more frequently than ever before. At the time, I didn’t realize those dreams were trying to send me a warning—an alarm I failed to understand.

Then one day, I saw him sick… and that sudden image shook me to my core. It pushed me to go home.

So, ten days ago, I returned to my family.

While coming back to Bangalore, I arrived at the airport around 11 PM. I booked a taxi through an app, expecting a normal ride back home. But in the middle of the night, the driver unexpectedly stopped the car and started demanding extra money. My heart raced. I was alone, vulnerable.

Without thinking, I called my father. He tracked my location and stayed on the phone with me the entire time, his voice filled with worry and fear, until I finally reached my destination safely. That night, I felt his deep concern as if he was guarding me from the shadows.

Back to present -

I booked an auto and reached the airport bus stand.

My bag felt heavier than it should, loaded not with clothes but with fear.

I stood there, sweating, scared, helpless… my eyes brimming silently with tears. Every breath uncertain.

That's when I saw her.

A fair-skinned girl, clearly not Indian, standing a few feet away. She looked equally lost—sapped by the heat, swallowed by the chaos.

Sara: "Is this the place for the airport bus?"

I looked up, trying to sound polite despite the storm inside me.

Me: "Yeah… I guess so."

Sara: "Okay… I'll wait here. It's too hot."

Her discomfort was palpable—perhaps from the oppressive heat, or the endless wait. Her face flushed. She pulled at her shirt, trying to cool herself.

Me: "Yeah. It's really dry today."

After a pause, I asked, "You're going to the airport?"

Sara: "Yeah… You too?"

Me: "Yeah."

We stood there, two strangers at a bus stop, caught between silence and an unspoken need for connection.

Sara: "It's been almost 15–20 minutes. No bus yet."

Me: "Yeah…"

Another pause. She seemed to weigh whether to trust me.

Sara: "Where are you headed?"

Me: "Chandigarh… My dad's in the hospital."

Her face softened, empathy blooming in her eyes.

Sara: "Oh… I'm so sorry."

Me: "Hmm…" I replied, almost absentmindedly.

Sara: "I'm Mumbai-bound. My flight's at 8 PM."

Me: "Okay."

Sara: "Do you work here, in Bangalore?"

Me: "Yes… at xyz company." I pointed across the road to the tall glass building. "That's my office."

Sara: "Ohh…"

An unexpected shift occurred—a quiet understanding bridging two strangers.

Perhaps it was my gentle tone, or the silent pain in my voice, but she seemed to lower her guard.

Me: “Let’s share a taxi?”

Sara: “Oh yeah… it’s too hot to wait now.”

I opened the uber taxi app. The driver was 10 minutes away.

As we waited, we talked—slowly, carefully, as if speaking would ward off the shadows circling us.

She told me about her time in Bangalore, her upcoming move. I shared small pieces of my story—just enough to keep the silence from overwhelming us.

For a fleeting moment, the crushing panic inside me faded… replaced by a fragile, shared humanity.

CHAPTER 4
A Stranger's Comfort

She sat in the front seat. I quietly slid into the back, not questioning her choice. Maybe she had motion sickness, maybe she just didn't want to get too friendly with a stranger—either way, I respected the silence.

I didn't say much. I couldn't. I stared out of the window, the city passing in a blur. It was a long ride—nearly an hour and a half to the airport—but it felt longer in my heart.

My thoughts spiraled.

What just happened to Papa? How did everything change so fast? Why am I on an emergency trip, unprepared and scared beyond words?

Tears welled up and quietly rolled down my cheeks.

She noticed. From the front seat, she turned slightly and asked gently,

"Do you need some water? Is everything okay?"

I wiped my face, forcing myself to speak.

"My dad… he had a brain haemorrhage. I'm flying to Chandigarh to be with him. I'm just praying he'll be okay."

She paused, then said softly,

"Don't worry. He's going to be fine."

Her voice carried calm. Reassurance. A kind of steadiness I didn't know I needed.

She asked a few more questions—when it happened, what symptoms he had—but I couldn't answer much. I didn't know the full picture myself. I was just rushing through the dark, hoping to catch up with the reality I hadn't even begun to understand.

And then she said something that stopped me.

"I'm a neurologist," she said.

"I handle brain haemorrhage patients."

I stared at her, stunned.

What were the odds? How could this be a coincidence—meeting a brain specialist right when I was drowning in fear and confusion about that exact thing?

She continued, calmly explaining things I hadn't yet processed.

"The brain works in reverse direction—your left hemisphere controls the right side of your body, and the right controls the left. That's why people with a left-sided brain bleed often lose strength on the right side."

I listened silently, absorbing each word like a lifeline.

"These cases are more common than people think. Nearly 30% of neurological emergencies are haemorrhagic. The good news? With timely intervention and ICU care, many recover well. The fact that your father reached the hospital on time—that's something to be grateful for."

I felt something shift inside. A drop of hope.

"The first 72 hours are the most critical," she added.

"That's when the risk of a second bleed is highest. But if he crosses that window… he has a strong chance of survival."

My breath slowed. My chest loosened. It felt like God had sent me someone—a stranger—to guide me through the first terrifying steps of this journey.

"I believe God is testing us," I whispered.

"He won't let anything happen. He can't. I trust him too much."

We reached the airport in silence after that—a comforting silence. She paid her share of the fare, smiled lightly, and wished me strength.

It was strange, but for the first time that day, I felt like maybe—just maybe—I wasn't completely alone. God is with me.

We stepped out of the cab and walked toward the airport departure gate. The sun was setting, and the heat still clung to the air like an unwelcome memory.

Me: "Oh wait—I forgot my idli parcel."

Sara: "What?"

Me: "I didn't eat anything since morning... too much going on."

She stopped and looked at me, her eyes kind but firm.

Sara: "Honey, you can't stay hungry like this."

Me: "It's okay... I'm not really hungry. But I could use some water."

Sara: "Let's get through check-in first, then we'll grab some."

We moved through the security lines. Everything around me was a blur—people, announcements, fluorescent lights—all meaningless noise against the weight in my chest.

We finally made it to Gate 21 and found two seats. She sat to my right, legs crossed, calm. I sat to her left, crumbling inside. Her flight was scheduled before mine—around 8 PM.

Me: "Do you think... my father will be okay? You're a neuro doctor, right?"

She looked at me gently, like someone sent with a purpose.

Sara: "Don't worry. This is meant to shake you—but not destroy you. He'll need time. Six to eight months, maybe... to be normal again."

Her words echoed and struck hard.

Normal.

Wasn't he normal just yesterday? Fit? Laughing? Smiling?

Me: "Fully recovered? Will he be the same?"

She hesitated.

Sara: "With brain haemorrhage... we can't promise that. He may struggle with speech, walking, daily routines. It all depends on how quickly he gets care."

The world seemed to tilt. I swallowed hard. It was like hearing about a stranger—not my father. How could someone so strong, so full of life, now be reduced to an "if"?

Sara: "Do you know which side was affected?"

I quickly dialed my sister.

Me: "Disha didi, which side was the stroke on?"

Disha didi : "Left."

Hung up.

Me: "Left side."

Sara smiled slightly.

Sara: "That's actually better news. Left-side strokes are tough, but not as critical as right-side ones. Don't panic. He's in the ICU, and that's where he should be right now."

I let out a shaky breath. My chest loosened for the first time all day.

Me: "Thank God... I needed to hear that."

Without a word, she got up, walked to a nearby kiosk, and returned with a bottle of water.

Sara: "Here. Drink this."

It felt like a small miracle.

Me: "He's at Aaman Hospital."

She pulled out her phone, typed something quickly.

Sara: "Hmm... not the best. It's actually more of a base camp for an army hospital."

My face must've shown the fear returning.

Me: "Is that... a bad sign?"

Sara: "For now, maybe not. But long term, you'll need to shift him to a specialized hospital with neurology facilities."

I nodded, heart pounding. My lips silently repeated the only prayer I knew.

Just then, my phone buzzed again.

Lakshay: "Where are you?"

Me: "Gate 21. You reached?"

Lakshay :"Yes. Heading to Gate 4."

I turned to sara.

Me: "Thank you. Really. I mean it."

Sara: "You'll be okay. Just don't lose hope."

We smiled—a silent goodbye. She disappeared toward her gate like she'd entered—suddenly, gently, like a message sent from above.

Maybe God had sent me this stranger to hold my hand through the storm I wasn't ready for.

***

At Gate 4

I walked to Gate 4. There stood my brother and his wife. He touched my feet—a rare gesture that felt heavier than it should. His face looked tired. Anxious. Like someone holding back a thousand thoughts.

He carried just a small bag. I noticed it—not packed for a long stay. Were we still hoping this was all temporary?

We boarded the flight.

The three of us were seated in the last row—seats kept specially for us.

For three hours, I sat there chanting Lord Shiva's name like a lifeline. Over and over again. If I could just do this—just hold my breath in prayer—maybe I could change fate. Maybe God would listen.

We landed in Chandigarh around midnight. My sister messaged me—she was outside, waiting with our cousin Rohit Bhaiya his name .

We stepped out, loaded our bags. Rohit Bhaiya placed mine carefully in the car's trunk. My sister sat in front, while we three squeezed into the backseat.

There was a strange calm in the Chandigarh air that night.

As if the city knew.

As if it was preparing to hold us through our toughest days

Rohit Bhaiya parked the car outside the hospital.

I stepped out, my heart thudding. I was desperate to see him... but terrified too. What if I couldn't bear to see him like that?

The building in front of us looked more like a rundown clinic than a hospital. Small. Dim. Almost lifeless.

I turned to my sister, unsettled.

"Is this really a hospital?" I asked. "It doesn't even look clean… It feels more like a local clinic. Not hygienic at all."

She nodded, "I know… I was so tensed. But papa insisted we bring him here. He had faith in this place. Said he'd recover only here before."

I exhaled sharply, frustrated and helpless. Instead of trusting logic, we had followed his faith.

"Where is he?" I asked.

"Third floor," Rohit bhaiya replied.

"In ICU, right?"

"Yes," sister said. "But they won't allow visitors right now. It's not the visiting hours."

"What?" I snapped. "He's my father. No one's stopping me." I was feeling mad actually.

We entered the lift. The air inside was thick with silence. As we reached the third floor, the doors opened to reveal a dimly lit corridor. The room marked ICU looked old, poorly maintained — nowhere close to the sterile space an ICU should be.

"This is the ICU?" I whispered. "This? This is where Papa is?"

I could feel my anger boil. He was a retired Army officer… he deserved better.he had that privilege to get treated in better place. He should've been taken to the best hospital in the city. Not this…

"Why did you bring him here?" I asked, almost shouting.

Sister spoke softly, "He chose it. He told us to come here… we just followed his wish."

I clenched my fists.

Outside the ICU, an elderly guard sat near the door. He had a clean-shaven face, a hat perched on his head, and deep wrinkles that made him look close to Papa's age — maybe 65 or more.

Rohit bhaiya approached him. "Uncle, please… they're his children. They've come from Bangalore. Let them see him."

Lakshay was the first to go in.

I was dying to see him. But something in me froze.

Do I have the courage to face him like this?

My legs felt like stone. My heart thudded against my ribs, trembling. I couldn't take a step forward… but I couldn't turn back either. I had to see him. I needed to.

After nearly 10 minutes of wrestling with my emotions, I forced myself to walk in.

There he was.

Lying on the ICU bed.

The right side of his body — paralyzed. Silent. Still.

I stood there, trying not to cry, not even a tear. Everyone — sara, the doctors — had told me the same thing: Don't show weakness in front of him.

He needed strength. I had to be that strength.

He slowly lifted his right hand with the help of his left — a trembling gesture that said everything.

It's not working, he was trying to tell me. He couldn't speak.

I held his hand. "It's okay, Papa. We're all here. You're going to be fine."

I couldn't stay longer than five minutes.

Just eleven days ago, I had seen him smiling, healthy, full of life. And now… this.

I walked out. My heart shattered, but my face — still dry. I had to be strong. For him.

CHAPTER 5
The Flashback

It was the end of the year, and I was in Bangalore.

The city had quietly wrapped itself in winter. The air was crisp, the evenings arrived earlier, and there was a tender chill that made you want to stay indoors. The nights stretched longer, darker, and strangely comforting. After a full day of work, I would collapse into bed, and sleep would come fast and deep—like the world outside had vanished.

Each morning, I'd wake to the scent of damp earth and soft air—that early winter fragrance that makes you pause, breathe, and feel alive.

But something inside me had begun to shift.

Almost every alternate night, I started dreaming of my grandmother and my elder brother. They have been passed away 2 years ago during winters. They would appear suddenly—sometimes just standing there, sometimes smiling faintly. Their presence wasn't frightening, but it left a heaviness in my chest when I woke. Was it a sign something? Were they trying to tell me something?

And then, the faces in my dreams began to change.

My father started appearing. Again and again.

Sometimes, he looked calm. Sometimes, in a hurry—like he was running late. And sometimes, he looked distant, silent, his eyes fixed on something I couldn't see.

The dreams didn't feel like dreams anymore. They felt like whispers—from somewhere I couldn't explain.

A thought began to haunt me: Is something going to happen?

A strange unease grew inside me, quiet but persistent. I didn't want to believe it, but deep down… I knew.

A storm was coming. Slowly, silently. And it was heading toward my door.

Then, one night, the dream turned darker—sharper.

I saw my father lying still, unable to move. His face was drawn tight with pain. He wasn't speaking—just lying there, helpless.

And we, his family, stood far away—watching, unable to help. The distance felt cruel.

I woke up with a jolt—panicked, breathless, drenched in sweat. My room felt colder than usual. The air was thick, as if something invisible and heavy was standing just beyond the door. I couldn't tell if it was the dream… or something that had followed me back from it.

Without thinking, I grabbed my phone and called my mother.

Me: "Hello?"

Mom: "Hello, beta?"

Me: "How's Papa? Is he okay?"

Mom: "He's fine. Why, what happened?"

Me: "I saw him in a dream. He looked unwell—in pain… helpless."

(A pause)

Mom: "Well… his feet have started swelling again."

My heart dropped.

My father had served in the Indian Army for years—stationed high in the frozen northern borders. That brutal cold had left its mark on him. Every winter, like a cruel ritual, his feet would swell painfully, old injuries and infections resurfacing like ghosts that refused to fade.

Me: "Can I talk to him?"

Mom: "He's not here right now, but I'll call him. Hold on."

A few minutes later, his familiar voice filled my ear—steady, strong… but softer than usual.

Papa: "Hello? How are you doing?"

Me: "I'm fine. But I saw you in my dream. You looked so weak. Are you sure you're okay?"

Papa: "Maybe because I think about you a lot these days… You're always on my mind."

Me: "Why do you think so much, Papa? Please don't worry about me."

Papa: "Because you're the last one I still carry in my heart as a responsibility. And I want to be free from that now."

Me: "What do you mean?"

Papa: "I've spent my life taking care of others. Now I just want peace. But I still think of you—wondering if you'll be alright."

His words hit me harder than I expected. It wasn't just concern. There was something deeper—something final—in his tone.

A quietness that sounded like farewell.

Me: "Please… don't say that. Everything will be okay."

Papa: "Hmm."

Silence stretched between us. We both knew we had more to say but didn't know how.

Me: "Papa, will you do something for me?"

Papa: "Tell me."

Me: "Please go to the temple this evening. Donate something—anything—on my behalf. Just pray. For strength. For peace. I don't know why, but I feel like something is coming."

He didn't question me. He just said softly,

"Okay, I will."

And that was it.

That same evening, he went to the temple—just as I had asked.

But after that, I began to notice something strange.

He was slowly pulling away—detaching himself from me, little by little. Why? He had never done that before. Was I imagining it? Or was he quietly preparing for something I couldn't see?

One morning, I called him about my two-wheeler license. His phone was busy. I waited, called again—still busy.

It had never happened before. My father always disconnected any ongoing call if I rang and called me back instantly. That's how much he worried about me.

But this time… he didn't.

Half an hour later, he finally answered. I wasn't angry—just confused.

Me: "Why didn't you call me back, Papa?"

Papa: "Is it necessary that I always have to be available for you?"

I froze.

That answer… it didn't sound like him.

No matter how much the world changes, a father never changes for his daughter. That's a truth I've always believed—God made fathers for the times He Himself couldn't be there.

And yet, mine was slipping away. Quietly. Silently.

The dreams didn't stop.

Every alternate night, I kept seeing him.

There was an energy at my door—unseen, uninvited, but there. Not loud. Just waiting.

January arrived in Bangalore. Winter lingered softly in the air.

And then, another dream.

I saw myself standing outside his room.

Inside, he was murmuring something—in pain. I couldn't reach him. I couldn't step in. I just stood there—helpless.

The dream clung to me long after I woke.

That morning, I knew.

I had to go.

I had to see him.

Somewhere deep inside, a voice whispered—

Go… or you'll regret it for the rest of your life.

I spoke to my sister and we decided to go together. Her kids would be on school vacation, so the timing felt right. I booked my flight for March 7th.

Days passed. Life went on.

One day, at the market, I thought, I'm earning well now. Why not buy something for Papa?

It's because of him that I am who I am. I wanted to gift him something special.

I bought a fine-quality pyjama and a warm jacket—expensive, elegant. I smiled to myself, imagining his reaction. He'd scold me for spending too much; he always hated unnecessary expenses.

But I already had an excuse ready—I'd tell him it was on discount from an end-of-winter sale.

CHAPTER 6

Home travel

I reached home on 7th March, early in the morning.

My sister came to pick me up with her kids.

But this time… he didn't come.

Usually, Papa would be the first to reach.

He'd hug me tight, smile wide, and ask, "How was the journey?"

But today, he stayed back.

Something inside me quietly noted that.

When I handed him the clothes I'd brought, he didn't react much—almost as if I'd wasted money. He said nothing.

Later, though, I saw him wearing the pajama. And when he did… a warmth spread through me. He had accepted it, even in silence.

But something felt off.

He was distant. Unreachable.

He didn't ask about my journey.

Didn't come to the station.

Didn't say much at all.

Why was he doing this?

A few days later, we took a small family trip—my sister, mother, the kids, and me.

Papa stayed home, alone.

It was meant to be a spiritual getaway, just for peace.

On the way, my mother murmured, almost to herself,

"I won't go anywhere anymore. Your father doesn't know how to manage the house or the kitchen without me."

Her words stayed with me.

Something about the way she said them—quietly, almost fearfully—felt strange.

After a few days, my sister returned; her kids had school.

And then it was just the three of us—Papa, Maa, and me.

For about a week, we stayed home together.

It was mid-March. Winter had nearly faded, but the evenings still carried a soft, whispering chill.

I loved cooking on the traditional clay stove—the slow, smoky way.

Papa would often sit beside me while I cooked. He talked a lot that week—about my marriage, about his business, about a family property dispute.

But I didn't want to hear any of it.

I kept thinking, Why is he talking like this? Why does he sound as if he's preparing me for something?

He's strong. He's here.

I didn't want to imagine a world without him.

Then came 18th March, around 4 PM.

I was packing my bag. My train was next morning.

My parents were having evening tea.

Suddenly, an urge rose inside me—to hug him.

I walked over, tears blurring my eyes, and said softly,

"You both are my world. I have no life beyond you. But still… you always give more attention to my siblings."

He looked up from his chair.

And for a moment, I saw it—his eyes widened, turned red, filled with something heavy.

He said nothing.

Just listened. Carefully. Silently.

As if each word I spoke was etching itself into his soul.

Maybe he was worried for me. Maybe… he already knew something I didn't.

I had left home before—many times.

But this time, my heart wouldn't stop crying.

Something inside me didn't want to go.

There was a strange stillness in the air.

The kind that doesn't feel peaceful.

The kind that feels like waiting.

The next morning, Papa came to drop me at the station—wearing the same jacket I'd gifted him.

That sight made me smile.

He never said much, but he always wore his love.

We took a few pictures together. Normally, he would scold me—

"Why do you keep taking pictures?"

But this time, he said nothing.

When the train arrived, he took out his old, dark brown wallet—thick and worn. I could see the familiar bulge of folded notes inside. He slowly pulled out several ₹500 notes, maybe around seven or eight thousand.

He wanted to give it all to me.

I said, half smiling,

"I do need it from you, Papa. You're the only provider in my life."

He didn't reply.

But his eyes were soft, helpless, full of a love that had no words.

It felt like he was saying, "This is all I can give you now."

That look still lives somewhere deep inside me.

I took a few notes—not because I needed them, but because it felt like my right.

He insisted on lifting my bag into the train, placing it in the luggage rack himself.

"Why are you doing this?" I said. "There are people here to help."

He looked at me—not with irritation, but with tenderness.

As if to say, "Because you're my child. My little girl. Always."

I hugged him tightly.

And then he stepped off the train.

Later, Maa told me that Papa cried a lot after coming home.

He said,

“If I’m not around, who will take care of her?”

Those words pierced straight through me.

That night, my flight to Bangalore was delayed.

By the time I landed, it was close to 11 PM.

The roads were dark and empty as I boarded a cab to my apartment.

The driver stopped midway to refuel—and something about him changed.

His tone turned sharp, his eyes strange. He began shouting, demanding money.

My heart was pounding.

I was terrified.

And in that moment, the only name that came to my lips was—Papa.

I called him immediately. He stayed awake the entire night, tracking my location, calling every few minutes.

Until I reached safely—2 AM.

That incident haunted him.

The next morning, he broke down. Cried uncontrollably.

He told Maa,

“I can’t rest. I keep thinking—if something happens to me, who will take care of her?”

From that day, he was never the same.

Restless. Unsettled.

He wanted just one thing—to see me safe, married, protected.

As if he knew his time with me was slipping away.

CHAPTER 7

The Night Everything Felt Broken

We came back to the hotel room—just around 200 meters away from the hospital.

The night air was cold, still. My heart was heavier than it had ever been.

Mom was already inside. As soon as I saw her, I broke down. I hugged her tightly and cried—cried for what had happened, for where we had landed, for how suddenly life had changed.

There was an ache inside me I couldn't describe. A sinking, trembling feeling. As if everything around us had collapsed.

Somewhere deep inside, a thought whispered: Have we done something wrong? Some sin, some curse… is this why we've reached here?

The hotel room was big, but it felt hollow. Just space filled with pain and confusion.

We hadn't eaten anything since morning. Finally, we ordered food—not out of hunger, but because we had to. Our bodies needed something, even if our hearts couldn't feel it.

We sat together, exhausted and broken, trying to make sense of the day.

Conversations turned into worried whispers. We all knew we had to be careful. In Indian hospitals, if attendants don't stay alert, doctors often don't pay enough attention. We had to be watchful. We couldn't afford to let anything slip.

The six of us sat quietly—me, Mummy, Disha didi, Lakshay , Purvi, and Rohit bhaiya.

We discussed the day—the ambulance, the reports, the word haemorrhage, the suddenness, the helplessness.

I was in deep pain—mentally, emotionally, physically. Part of me still kept praying, Please let this be a dream. Let me wake up from this nightmare.

But this was no dream. This was our new reality.

It was already past 3 AM.

We knew we couldn't all fit in the same room, so we divided ourselves.

Me, Disha didi, and Purvi would sleep on the double bed.

Mummy would take the extra mattress on the floor.

Rohit bhaiya and Lakshay decided to go to a relative's house a bit far in Kharar bit away 10-15 km —just for the night.

Even though my body begged for sleep, my mind wouldn't allow it. I lay on the bed beside Mummy, trying to close my eyes—but every time I did, my thoughts screamed louder.

I knew I had to rest. Tomorrow was going to be a tough day. We had to speak to the doctor, understand the full analysis, hear the truth face-to-face. Somehow, I forced myself into a shallow, uneasy sleep.

Morning came too soon.

Around 7 AM, the doorbell rang. Purvi opened it. Rohit bhaiya and Lakshay stood outside. Everyone got up, though no one had really slept.

There wasn't a moment to waste.

We all started getting ready quickly. The hospital had allowed visiting time by 9 AM.

In between the chaos, I called Sara to update her. She listened patiently, guiding me step by step—what to do next, how to speak to the doctor, what to observe.

"Check his reports, understand his medications, observe his consciousness. Can he open his eyes? How wide? What kind of movements does he show? Send everything back to me," she said.

Meanwhile, she said she'd check the neurologist's qualifications at the hospital—whether we needed to shift Papa somewhere better.

I nodded. Agreed.

And in that moment, something shifted inside me.

I realized—I had no space to break down anymore. No room for emotion. If I collapsed now, everything would fall apart.

I had to stay strong.

We left the hotel promptly by 8:30, desperate to reach the hospital early. No one wanted to lose a single second—we needed to see him, to be near him.

A long queue awaited us. But we stood silently, united in urgency.

I walked behind everyone, my steps heavy, my heart heavier. My legs moved, but my mind refused to accept what was happening. Something tragic had struck, and I wasn't ready for it. I wasn't prepared.

We took the lift together—old, creaky, painfully slow. Buttons barely worked, stiff and unresponsive, stopping at almost every floor. I remember thinking: What if someone's in a rush? These stops would only add panic.

A part of me wanted to take the stairs, just to avoid the suffocating ride, to move faster. But I couldn't. My legs felt like they carried the weight of the world. Each step would have felt like dragging a mountain.

We believe our fathers are superheroes—invincible, full of energy, larger than life. They never grow weak, never grow old. At least, that's what we tell ourselves.

I remembered working in Gurgaon, traveling late at night, sometimes reaching the bus stop at midnight—or even 3 AM. I never once felt afraid. Never worried about getting home. Because I knew, without fail, one man would be there waiting for me. My superhero. Papa. Standing at the bus stop, no matter how late, ready to walk me home.

And now, that same superhero lay in a hospital bed, struggling to even speak. Was this really happening?

Finally, we reached the ICU.

The worn-out hospital only deepened my sense of helplessness. The guard said only one person could enter at a time.

Seven of us were there—me, Mummy, Disha didi, Lakshay, Purvi, Rohit bhaiya and Gyan Uncle, Papa's friend who had just arrived.

Tension hung between us. Everyone hesitated.

We eventually decided to go in two at a time.

I was desperate to see him, to be near him—but I couldn't.

My body refused to move.

My heart shattered into pieces.

And I stood there—paralyzed by fear, by love, by grief.

CHAPTER 8
Hospital Journey

Hospital – Day 2

I was the last to enter the hospital.

Each step felt heavier than the last, my heart pounding so loud it drowned out every sound around me.

I was terrified—

Terrified of seeing him like that.

As I stepped inside, I froze.

There he was—Bed No. 1.

My father.

He lay straight, draped in a lime-green, lined hospital gown.

But he wasn't still. His body kept shifting—slightly, restlessly—as though he was fighting his own breath.

Because one side of him… was already gone.

Paralysed.

He was relying on the other half of his body to survive—to breathe. Each inhale came fast and shallow, each exhale sharp and desperate, like his lungs were battling against time itself.

He was gasping.

Fighting.

Surviving.

His eyes were wide open—staring.

I remembered Sara's words echoing in my head:

"If his eyes are open, it's a good sign."

I clung to that sentence like a lifeline made of thread.

But the rest of him… was slipping away.

The left side of his mouth hung low, motionless.

He couldn't speak.

He tried—God, he tried.

I saw the faint tremble of his lips, the desperate strain in his neck—

But no words came out.

Just yesterday, he was talking.

Today, he couldn't even open his mouth.

His breathing grew faster.

Too fast.

I searched his face for any sign of recognition—any flicker of awareness in those once sharp, commanding eyes.

Nothing.

No response. No movement. No gesture that said he knew we were there.

He was there… but not fully there.

Trapped inside his own body.

Fighting a war no one could fight for him.

Beside him, a small hospital table stood neatly—his chart clipped on top, a few papers fluttering under the fan. His IV line dripped clear fluid into his veins, marking time in tiny, cruel drops.

But I couldn't absorb any of it.

All I could see was him.

My father.

The man who raised us with iron discipline and unshakable strength.

A retired Army officer.

A protector.

A pillar.

And now… this.

How could someone so strong—so alive—be lying there so helpless?

No one prepares you for this moment.

The moment your protector becomes the one who needs protecting.

As children, we never really believe our parents will grow old.

They're our constants—our forever.

I remembered one night from years ago, when I used to travel late from Gurgaon. I had reached home near midnight.

Mother had said softly, "Don't come so late, beta. Try to reach earlier next time."

I had laughed, "Why?"

She looked at me gently and said, "Your father is getting old now."

I had laughed again. "Old? He doesn't look it."

Back then, it felt impossible.

Parents don't age. Not ours.

Not the father who once stood guard for the country.

Not the man who carried our entire world on his shoulders.

And yet—there he was.

Fragile. Silent. Struggling.

I tried speaking to the doctors—asking every question Sara had told me to ask.

But no one had answers.

No one had clarity.

"We have to wait for the neurologist," they said. "Dr. Ruhi will be here by 1 PM."

It was 9:30 AM. Visiting hours were already over.

Everyone was drained—physically, emotionally.

We had nowhere to rest. No waiting area. No spare beds for attendants.

Hotels nearby were too expensive. We didn't even know how long we'd be here.

After a long discussion, we finally decided—

Mom, Disha didi, Purvi, and Gyan Uncle would go home.

I, Rohit Bhaiya, and Lakshay would stay back.

Disha didi objected.

"You're too emotional," she said. "You won't be able to handle seeing him like this."

But I stood firm.

"No. I'll stay. Even if it means sleeping on the hospital floor—I'll stay."

Because I knew myself.

If someone else called to update me about him, I wouldn't survive it.

I needed to see everything with my own eyes.

Somewhere deep inside, something whispered—

He needs you.

Lakshay wasn't the talkative kind. Rohit bhaiya went quiet in tense moments.

But me?

I would speak.

I would question.

And if the doctors failed him, I would fight.

I couldn't trust second-hand words.

I trusted only what my eyes saw.

It was almost noon when we checked out of the hotel.

We were still waiting for the neurologist.

The rest of the family decided they would leave after meeting her.

But time passed.

1 PM came and went.

Still… no doctor.

Panic started to build inside me—slow, suffocating.

How could a doctor be so careless?

This wasn't a normal case.

This was a brain haemorrhage.

Did they not understand what was at stake?

I kept going to the reception, again and again, asking for her full name.

Nobody knew.

Everyone only called her Dr. Ruhi.

But I wanted more.

I wanted to know who she was—her qualifications, her experience, her background—

Because this woman now held my father's fate in her hands.

CHAPTER 9

Doctor Talk

Hospital – Day 2 (Continued)

It was almost 2 PM when Dr. Ruhi finally arrived.

We all rushed toward her, desperate—starving—for answers.

Yesterday, no one had told us anything.

They'd said they needed to "run tests" first.

So today, she was our last thread of hope.

But the moment I saw her, my heart sank.

She looked so young. Too young.

Barely out of college.

My thoughts started spiraling—

Is she even experienced enough?

How can someone so young handle something this serious?

Why is this happening to us?

It wasn't just doubt. It was fear.

I didn't trust her.

Not with my father's life.

I started firing questions—every single one Sara had told me to remember.

One after another, like a checklist I clung to for sanity.

She answered calmly, her voice steady…

But her words—each one—landed like a knife.

> "We can't say anything right now. We have to wait. These 70 hours are very critical."

Seventy hours.

It felt endless.

Like someone had chained us to a chair and told us to watch him suffer—minute by minute—without being able to do a thing.

She went on, clinically.

> "His BP is very high. We're doing everything, but it isn't coming down. That's making things more risky."

"He's struggling to breathe."

"And yes… he has a history of daily alcohol intake. That's working against him now."

And then came the words that broke something inside me—

"There's bleeding… hemorrhage… in almost every critical area of his brain."

For a second, I stopped breathing.

I wanted to close my eyes and open them 70 hours later, when it was all over.

But this wasn't a nightmare.

It was real.

And I was wide awake inside it.

By evening, Mom, Disha Didi, Gyan Uncle, and Purvi left for home—emotionally and physically drained.

It was just me, Rohit Bhaiya, and Lakshay now.

We sat on the hospital stairs for hours—sometimes talking, sometimes staring at the tiles in silence.

The kind of silence that hums with pain.

We went to see Papa three, maybe four times.

We didn't go far.

We just stood outside the ICU glass window, refusing to leave sight of him.

Part of it was fear—

If the doctors or nurses thought no one was watching, would they still give him the same care?

We couldn't take that risk.

***

Around 8 PM, we went again.

Dr. Prakash was on duty this time.

His voice was sharp, his tone cutting.

Maybe that's just how he spoke—but to us, in that moment, it felt cruel.

> "He's struggling to breathe," he said flatly.

"He's using all his strength on just one side. We might have to put him on a ventilator tomorrow."

That word—ventilator—hit like a bullet to the chest.

I felt cold.

Empty.

Like someone had drained the world of sound.

***

That night, Rohit Bhaiya dropped me at one of his relatives' homes nearby.

It wasn't comfortable. It wasn't home.

I didn't even want to go—but I had to.

He and the others went to stay at another relative's house in Karnal, about 10–15 km away.

My mind wouldn't stop.

Thoughts kept looping like a broken record—

Let these 72 hours pass. Please.

Just let him survive, and then I'll move him to a better hospital.

I made up my mind right there:

Tomorrow, I'd visit Sobha, Max, Fortis—every hospital I could find.

I'd talk to every senior neurologist in the city.

If there was even one chance to save him, I'd take it.

We discussed it all day—it was the only thing that gave us a sense of control.

A plan.

A reason to breathe.

***

Later that night, lying in that unfamiliar room, I prayed silently.

Thank you, God.

You've stayed with us this far.

We've made it through 48 hours. Please… let tomorrow go well. Let us cross that 72-hour mark. Let him be out of danger.

I knew I had two battles to fight now.

One—with myself—

To see him like that and still not fall apart.

And the other—with the world—

To question, to push, to make sure the doctors didn't fail him.

Because now… I wasn't just his daughter.

I was his soldier.

And I had no choice but to fight.

CHAPTER 10

Between Life and Breath

It was 6 o'clock in the morning.

The air was mildly chilled — the kind that brushes against your skin like a quiet warning.

I felt happy… or maybe just relieved.

Only 24 hours left. Just 24 hours, and he would be out of danger.

"Thank you, God," I whispered. "I know You're with me. You've tested us, but You've never abandoned us. You protect in strange ways."

Just one more day.

If I could close my eyes and open them tomorrow at this same hour, maybe everything would be okay.

We would've crossed the finish line.

We would've won.

I got ready faster than I ever had in my life. I wanted to reach the hospital early, to meet Dr. Shubham — the neurosurgeon. He usually came between 8:30 and 9:30 a.m. I couldn't afford to miss him. Not today.

I had never handled anything like this before. I'm the fragile one — emotional, soft, easily shaken. Everyone knew that.

Disha didi always used to joke, "If we keep her in a hospital to handle something like this, we'll need another bed just for her."

And she wasn't wrong. I had fainted once — and that was for a minor issue.

And now, this.

At the reception, I asked about Dr. Subham. The lady said gently, "He'll come anytime, ma'am. He recently operated on a neurosurgery case."

It was 9 a.m. already. There was a long queue outside the ICU — faces swollen with sleeplessness and grief. The air was thicker today, heavier, filled with something unspoken.

A woman was crying silently near the wall. Her father was also inside icu. I knew what she felt — that wordless pain that only daughters understand.

Watching the man who once carried you on his shoulders now lying helpless, wired, and still — it's like watching your world collapse in slow motion.

Your hero, defeated.

The guard uncle didn't stop us today. He'd seen us for two days straight — seen our pain, our trembling, our silent pleading.

Inside, Papa was gasping. Only his right side moved — the left had gone completely still.

It looked like half his body had forgotten how to live.

Then came the moment that cracked my soul.

On duty doctor dr Neha approached me with a clipboard. "Ma'am," she said softly, "we need you to sign the consent form. We have to put him on a ventilator."

My hands froze.

"Ventilator?" I repeated. "Why?"

She looked calm — too calm. "He's struggling to breathe."

My throat tightened. "No. You can't just do that! I need to speak to the doctor. Sara told me clearly — not a single step without the main doctor's approval."

The duty doctor stepped in. "Ma'am, night doctor already informed you last night, right?"

His words hit like a slap.

Something was wrong — deeply wrong.

Papa's case was covered under army insurance — all treatment was free. So why the rush? Why the pressure? Was this about saving him or saving money?

Inside, a voice whispered — They're doing this for a reason that isn't yours.

I called Sara. My voice shook as I told her everything.

"Something's off," she said immediately. "Don't let them do anything until you talk to the main doctor."

I nodded, but my body was trembling. I didn't know what was right anymore. I just knew I couldn't lose him.

Not like this. Not in some cold room full of strangers and machines.

We rushed to the reception to speak to Dr. Ruhi on phone.

"She's refused to speak to you," the receptionist said.

"What?"

My voice broke. "Why?"

Because I had questioned her qualifications? Because I had dared to ask too many questions?

Frustration burned through me.

Hospitals are supposed to heal, not humiliate.

When families break, doctors are supposed to hold them — not hide behind silence.

I demanded to speak with Dr. Sampak, the hospital head. He tried calling her too.

She didn't answer. Not even for him.

That was it. I broke.

We were three shattered people — me, Lakshay, and Rohit bhaiya — running between corridors like ghosts, clutching nothing but hope.

"God," I whispered, "I'll fight anyone, I'll do anything — just save him."

My chest was a storm. My body felt like paper.

Three days ago, he was laughing.

Now he was barely breathing.

A nurse in a navy-blue uniform pulled me aside.

"If you delay," she said flatly, "it'll be on you. If we don't put him on now, he might not make it. But once he's on, it'll be very hard to bring him back. The body forgets how to fight."

Her words tore through me.

Put him on — lose him slowly.

Don't put him — lose him suddenly.

What kind of choice is that?

I could barely breathe. I wanted to run. Scream. Pray.

Anything.

We sat on the staircase, all three of us, motionless.

It was 11 a.m.

Dr. Ruhi wouldn't come until 2.

And then, out of nowhere, a girl in white handed me a phone.

"Ma'am," she said softly, "someone wants to talk to you."

It was her — Dr. Ruhi.

Her voice was calm, clinical. "He's struggling to breathe. If we wait, he could go into multi-organ failure. We have to put him on the ventilator."

She paused. Then said quietly, "He's been consuming alcohol for years. His body is reacting. We have to control it. His BP is too high.

That one line — that small clarity — made me stop resisting.

I signed.

At 12 p.m., we were called in.

Papa lay still. Machines were breathing for him now.

But he looked peaceful. For the first time in last few hours, his face wasn't fighting.

Lakshay said softly, "At least now he looks relaxed."

I nodded.

For the first time, it didn't look like pain had won — just that he was resting after a long battle.

We went to a small dhaba across the road. Ate in silence.

The tea was bitter. The world was numb.

We talked about shifting him, about hope, about the hours left — fifteen more, that's all we needed.

Fifteen hours more of strength, breath, and faith.

CHAPTER 11

Clinging to Hope

We were counting the minutes till 2 o'clock — the moment we could finally speak to Dr. Ruhi.

It was the 3rd of April. The summer heat had started to creep in — thick, sticky, almost cruel.

The sun glared down with the kind of weight that pressed against your chest, adding to the anxiety already tightening every breath.

All we could talk about was Papa's recovery — how long it might take, how hard it would be.

But as I sat there, my mind began wandering into strange corners.

What if the heat makes it worse for him?

What if shifting him adds to his discomfort?

Ridiculous, right? But fear makes logic evaporate. It eats you alive from the inside, in quiet, irrational ways.

Then—Lakshay's phone rang.

I hadn't even given the hospital my number.

My stomach dropped. My blood froze.

Why were they calling? What had happened?

I didn't want to know. I didn't want to hear it.

My whole body screamed, What if this is it? What if something terrible's happened?

We rushed to the hospital.

I spotted Dr. Ruhi from a distance — calm, composed, untouched by the chaos that lived inside me.

She didn't mention the tension from that morning. She just began explaining things, her voice steady, professional, detached — like this was just another day at work.

She told me the hemorrhage had occurred in the thalamus — the most critical, central part of the brain.

I didn't fully understand what it meant. But I could feel from her tone… it was serious. Very serious.

"He has swelling and internal bleeding," she said.

"We're waiting for seventy-two hours to pass — to see if another attack comes.

If he survives that, we can consider it a win."

Then she added softly —

"He used to drink daily. His body's demanding it now. We're trying to control it with multivitamins and monitoring him constantly, but the withdrawal itself can be dangerous."

She spoke of blood pressure, medication, brain swelling — the fragile line between survival and surrender.

And I listened, every word cutting deeper than the last.

I wanted to say sorry for the morning — for questioning her, for doubting her.

But I couldn't. Because she had failed me too.

When I was breaking apart, she had treated me like a nuisance.

And all I was… was a daughter trying to save my father.

Afterward, I went to the reception and collected Papa's medical summary.

We were planning to visit Shobha Hospital — for a second opinion.

Maybe for some hope. Maybe just for strength.

As we reached Shobha's massive gates, something inside me twisted.

The hospital was huge — spotless, organized, serene.

And I couldn't stop wondering, What if we had brought him here from the start? Would he be in a better state now?

At the reception, I begged to meet a neurologist.

I was willing to pay anything — I just wanted someone to look at the file.

But the doctor refused.

"Bring the patient first," he said coldly. "Only then will we talk."

I pleaded. Begged.

"Please, just look at the summary once. Tell me if he can be treated better."

But he was unmoved — arrogant, dismissive.

And that's when something inside me broke.

Are doctors really healers anymore?

Or have their degrees become crowns they wear to distance themselves from pain?

I wanted to scream. To break past security.

To throw that file in front of him and yell — This is my father, not just another case number!

Outside, I called my cousin's husband — he's a doctor. He offered to forward the reports to a neurologist friend.

I thanked him, but deep down, I felt hollow.

Defeated. Betrayed.

That day, a bitter truth took root in me —

Medicine, at least in India, had become business.

And patients with insurance? We were nothing more than gold-laying hens.

By 5 p.m., we were back at Aaman Hospital. Visiting hours.

Papa was still unconscious, lying on ICU Bed No. 1.

A thick white pipe was down his throat, connected to the ventilator.

Beside him, a giant monitor flashed with lines and numbers I couldn't understand.

I took out my phone to record the screen — I thought I'd Google it later.

But before I could, a nurse came running.

"Ma'am! You can't do that! It's against policy. We've already given you the summary!"

She scolded me like I was committing a crime.

But I wasn't. I was just a desperate daughter trying to hold on to whatever little control I had left.

I walked out, my heart pounding, my soul aching.

We crossed the road to the same small dhaba.

The sun had softened, but the fire inside me hadn't.

We sat there in silence — restless, afraid, counting hours.

We kept whispering like a prayer —

Just twelve more hours.

Just twelve hours and he'll cross the danger mark.

As if repeating it could make it true.

We weren't waiting for a miracle anymore.

We were clinging to it.

That night, I was supposed to stay at Rohit Bhaiya's relative's house nearby, while he and Lakshay stayed in Kharar, 10-15 kilometers away.

I felt awkward — guilty even — about staying too long in someone else's home.

But we needed to be close to the hospital. Papa's recovery, we thought, could take time.

So we stayed a little late, planning to see him from outside the ICU before leaving.

We sat at that same little dhaba again — our waiting place — talking endlessly about the doctors, the treatment, our regrets.

Each word was a thread of fear, guilt, and helplessness tangled together.

By 9 p.m., we walked back to the ICU.

The guard uncle at the door had stopped stopping us.

Maybe he sensed it — the grief, the love, the heaviness in our eyes.

Maybe he understood.

Through the glass, I saw him.

Papa.

Lying there — motionless. Unconscious.

Oh God… I never imagined I would see you like this.

You were my Superman — the man who could fix anything, do anything.

How could this happen to you?

My chest tightened. My mind screamed.

I wasn't ready for this. I couldn't be.

My brother quietly took my hand and led me downstairs.

My tears had stopped — not because the pain was gone, but because it was too heavy to cry.

It just sat there — sharp, merciless — slicing through my heart like a slow, unending knife.

Just one night, I told myself.

Just one night, and tomorrow we'll be closer to recovery.

That was the hope I clung to.

Even though, deep down…

a shadow of fear had already begun to spread.

CHAPTER 12

The Morning That Lied to Me

It was 4th April, around 6:30 a.m., when I woke up.

For the first time in days, there was a faint smile on my face — a strange sense of relief, as if someone had just announced, "We've won the war. No one can defeat us now. Even God Himself has given His word."

It felt like the universe had finally paused its cruelty — as if this had only been a test, and the message was clear:

"I will not harm your father anymore."

The reason for my confidence was simple — we had crossed the dreaded 72-hour mark without another attack. In my head, that was victory. Now, all that remained was recovery.

Four days.

Four days of living in a nightmare that had stripped me of everything — my identity, my sleep, my hunger, even my sense of time.

The world outside had stopped existing.

All that remained were a few fixed words echoing in my head:

Aaman Hospital. ICU. 3rd Floor. Bed No. 1. My father on it.

I had never felt pain so raw, so merciless. It felt like my heart had been placed on an anvil and struck, again and again, just to test how much it could endure.

Still, that morning, I called my mother and Disha didi.

I congratulated them. Told them we had crossed the toughest phase. I wanted them to breathe easier, even if I couldn't.

Inside, I felt a fragile satisfaction — the kind that trembles in your chest like a flicker of light in a storm.

At 9 a.m., it was time for the ICU visit.

My legs trembled, my chest tightening with every step. The elevator ride to the 3rd floor always felt like being pulled toward a place you feared but couldn't avoid.

I hated being the first to enter — that first sight always broke something inside me.

And there he was.

Still unconscious. Still on the ventilator.

But at least — at least — he wasn't gasping anymore.

That morning, Dr who was on duty, his face already drawn with irritation. He reminded me sharply that he had explained the ventilator decision last night and demanded to know why I had "created a scene."

We argued.

"I've seen my father walking, talking, laughing. You expect me to accept this in one night?" I told him, my voice trembling. "I'm not in control of these emotions, sir. I just want him back."

I confessed that I came from an different background of education—and right now I dont understand your medical terms, only emotions.

And they had said themselves — Once on a ventilator, it's very difficult to take someone off it.

He shoved a paper toward me, asked me to write down a term to prove I understood. My hands were shaking too much. He told me to stop interrupting if I didn't.

But how could I?

I kept taking photos of the ventilator secretly, desperate to decode what was happening. The nurses caught me again, scolding me for my behavior.

The moment I stepped out of the ICU, I called Sara.

I needed comfort.

Instead, her tone froze me — cold, flat, detached.

She told me now that Papa was on a ventilator, the next step would be inserting a tube through his neck — a direct line to the lungs. And then, slowly, his heart would give out.

She said it as if she were preparing me.

Her words slammed into me like bullets.

What was she saying?

Why did she sound like she was enjoying scaring me?

Just yesterday, she had been a well-wisher. Today, she felt like an enemy.

We were supposed to be past the danger — we had crossed the three most critical days. Right?

We walked toward the reception.

That's when I saw him.

A tall, sharply dressed man — around forty-five, handsome, calm, exuding quiet authority.

Someone had once told me: Dr. Shubham is very handsome — mid-aged, but magnetic.

It had to be him.

Without thinking, I rushed toward him.

Dr. Shubham had operated on a man with brain bleeding, and he often visited his patient in the ICU. That morning, I waited outside, holding on to a sliver of hope — maybe, if I could just talk to him, he'd say something to calm the storm inside me.

When the ICU doors opened and he stepped out, I felt a strange gravity in his presence — the kind that made you believe every word he said.

I asked about Papa.

He looked at me, and his tone shifted — slow, grave, measured.

He explained that because of Papa's age and the location of the bleeding, things were extremely dangerous.

The thalamus, he said, was the center of the brain — a place you never wanted damaged.

And then he said it.

"Your father is fighting with death as of now."

The words didn't just hit my ears — they stabbed straight into my chest.

I froze. My mind went blank.

My God… I had thought he was recovering. That we had crossed the danger zone.

But here was the expert — telling me we were still inside it.

For a moment, I couldn't even stand. My knees weakened, the corridor tilted, the air thickened.

My thoughts spiraled: Have I done something wrong? Is this punishment?

I wanted to scream, to tear the pain out of my chest, but all I could do was stand still — hollow, trembling, numb.

The rest of the day passed in a haze.

I sat glued to my phone, typing every term I could remember — thalamus, brain hemorrhage, ventilator, survival rate, probability of recovery.

Each search result cut a little deeper.

But I couldn't stop.

Because somewhere between science and faith, I was still searching for one word —

Hope.

CHAPTER 13

When Silence Became His Voice

It was the fifth day of living in the same unbearable emotional storm.

I had thought the first four days were the hardest of my life — but this… this was worse.

Papa lay unconscious in the ICU, trapped somewhere between life and death, his body kept alive by the hiss and hum of the ventilator.

The machine was breathing for him — a mechanical rhythm that sounded like mercy but felt like cruelty.

He looked strangely peaceful, almost as if sleeping… but I knew better. It was an artificial calm — the kind that comes from surrender, not rest.

Every detail of his decline was recorded neatly in a blue hospital file — that file had become my greatest fear.

That morning, my eyes caught the number written beside "Temperature": 400.

My heart stopped.

I didn't need a doctor to explain it. A fever that high was no coincidence. It was a warning — loud, merciless, and real.

His blood pressure refused to settle. I knew that was how it had all begun — dangerously high BP that had detonated inside his brain like a silent bomb.

Papa had been an alcoholic — a common shadow in the lives of army men. It had been his habit, his escape, his quiet poison.

Now, that same poison was fighting him from the inside.

The nurses wrapped his arms and feet in white, water-soaked bandages, changing them every hour, waiting for Dr. Ruhi's rounds between 1:30 and 2:30 p.m.

The on-duty doctor said softly, "He's on full ventilator support. The machine is doing everything for him. He seems relaxed."

But I knew why he looked relaxed — because he wasn't there.

Every time he regained even a flicker of consciousness, he would fight — pulling at the ventilator, trying to tear the tube from his throat, as if his body still remembered freedom even when his mind didn't.

And I… I just stood there.

Helpless. Watching. Breaking.

They took him for CT scans again and again, chasing the same shadows — swelling, blood clots, damaged nerves. The clot had blocked a major pathway in his brain, cutting off blood supply and paralyzing the entire left side of his body.

Every drug, every treatment, every decision — all of it went into that blue file.

But I wasn't allowed to read it.

It was his life in those pages, yet I had no right to open them.

I could feel it — they were hiding something. But I swallowed my questions. I couldn't afford to offend anyone. My father's life depended on their mercy.

Still, one thought haunted me — this wasn't just medicine.

This was business.

Hospitals today don't see pain. They see potential billing.

You stop being a person the moment you step inside — you become a number, a policy, a walking invoice.

***

We decided to rent a room near the hospital — not just for convenience, but for sanity.

Those endless hours sitting on plastic chairs, breathing antiseptic air thick with fear and disinfectant — it was enough to drive anyone mad.

We found a small room just 150 meters away, tucked in a narrow lane beside the hospital.

An elderly Punjabi couple, uncle and aunty, lived there. They were in their sixties — warm eyes, kind hearts.

The room wasn't much, but it was shelter. A place to collapse. A place to cry where no one could see.

That same day, Papa's elder brother came to visit.

On the surface, it looked like concern. But I knew — deep down — it wasn't.

Old property disputes had poisoned their bond years ago. I later realized that the stress of those fights had eaten away at Papa's peace, his health, maybe even pushed him closer to this.

In that sterile hospital corridor, I learned something cruel:

Even blood ties can be counterfeit.

***

Days bled into one another.

The sixth, seventh, and eighth days — all the same.

No improvement. No decline. Just waiting.

Each morning brought the same reports: temperature fluctuating, blood pressure unstable, scans repeated, medicines changed.

Doctors said they were managing his alcohol withdrawal with multivitamins and close observation — but none of it felt like hope.

We were existing, not living.

Running on fumes, surviving on caffeine, prayers, and denial.

Relatives called, each bringing a different remedy, a different god.

Some urged us to keep reciting Sundarkand Path, calling it the most powerful prayer.

Others told us to visit temples, to light lamps, to promise offerings.

But deep down, all I wanted was for him to open his eyes — even for a second — and look at me.

Papa lay there, utterly still.

No response. No movement. No awareness.

It felt like watching the shell of a man who once filled every room with laughter.

And in those silent hours, guilt began to eat me alive.

In the rush of my professional life, I had visited less, called less, assumed there would always be more time.

Now, all I wanted was one more day with him. One more conversation. One more chance to say thank you.

Fathers have a language of love that daughters often learn too late.

They don't say I love you — they show it in actions, in the way they fix what's broken, protect without words, and carry your pain like it's their own.

And when they fall, the world loses its balance.

So, we waited.

For another day. Another hour. Another miracle.

Because sometimes, waiting is the only thing left when hope refuses to die.

CHAPTER 14
Breaking Point

Nine days.

Nine endless, punishing days of hearing the same words on repeat — critical… can't say anything… anytime, anything can happen.

Every morning it was the same ritual. The doctors walked in, repeated their well-rehearsed lines, and slid another paper toward us to sign — a form stating we understood that my father could leave us at any moment.

By now, my signature felt cursed — a daily reminder that death was still hovering above us.

That morning, something inside me broke.

I grabbed my phone and called Maa.

"Why did you even bring Papa to this hospital?" My voice trembled, half rage, half helplessness. "Every single day they say the same thing — critical, critical, critical — and I see no improvement. They're just stretching it out, Maa. They're bleeding us dry, waiting for the insurance to finish. They don't care about Papa… they only care about money!"

There was silence on the other end before she spoke, her voice soft but worn out.

"Your father trusted this hospital. That's why we brought him here."

"Trust?" I almost laughed. "I don't see trust here, Maa. I see business. They're treating him like a number, not a person."

She sighed. "Fine. I'll come. I'll talk to them myself. I'll tell them — we have faith in you, please save him."

But I wasn't waiting anymore.

My chest burned with anger, fear, and the ache of nine sleepless nights. I stormed through the corridors and went straight to the cabin of Dr. Sankalp — the hospital owner.

"I want a progress report," I said, my voice shaking. "No more vague words. No more 'critical.' Tell me what's really happening."

He looked at me calmly, choosing his words with care.

He said the bleeding was in a dangerous area, that recovery couldn't be fast, that we needed patience. His tone was polite — but I could hear the subtext: Don't expect a miracle.

"If you can't do anything," I cut him off, "tell me right now. I'll take him somewhere else."

He hesitated, promised to "get back to me," but I'd had enough.

I went straight to Lakshay and Rohit bhaiya. "We're shifting him. Enough is enough."

They nodded — exhausted, defeated, desperate.

We went to the reception and demanded his medical summary. I didn't care how loud I sounded. My father's life was not a file to be tucked away in a drawer.

The Call

It came suddenly.

No warning. No preparation.

Lakshay's phone rang — not mine, because I'd never given the hospital my number.

The look on his face made my stomach twist.

We rushed to the ICU.

The on-duty doctor met us halfway, his tone urgent but calm. He said they needed to perform a tracheostomy — a new ventilator tube through Papa's neck instead of his mouth. I didn't fully understand, but at that moment, medical terms meant nothing. We nodded. We just wanted him to survive.

That evening, at exactly 5 p.m., we headed for our routine ICU visit.

And that's when I saw him.

The guard uncle — in his navy-blue uniform, black cap tilted forward — was standing near the ICU doors. But this time, he wasn't just smiling politely. His face was lit up, eyes gleaming, as if he carried some divine secret.

I slowed down, trying to read his expression.

Why was he smiling like that?

He leaned closer and whispered,

"Sir has opened his eyes."

For a moment, the words didn't make sense.

Then they sank in.

He opened his eyes.

My heart leapt. My vision blurred. My hands trembled. I could feel something warm rush through me — disbelief, gratitude, joy — all at once.

"Oh God… thank you," I whispered, my voice breaking. "Thank you, thank you…"

For nine long days, I had been drowning in darkness — and suddenly, there was light.

We rushed inside the ICU. The doctor confirmed it: Papa had opened his eyes.

He was conscious — breathing through the new tube, still surrounded by machines — but alive, aware, present.

Even with all those wires and tubes around him, when he looked at us, it felt like life itself had returned to the room.

I wanted to cry, to scream, to fall to my knees and thank the heavens.

It felt like someone had breathed life back into a lifeless doll — and it moved again.

The doctor told us they would begin reducing the ventilator support, letting him breathe more on his own. Slowly. Carefully. Preparing to take him off it entirely.

For the first time in days…

I believed.

Maybe — just maybe — we were going to bring him home.

CHAPTER 15

The First Smile After Nine Days

10 April — Morning, 9:00 AM

We were going to see Papa.

For the first time in nine days, I didn't feel that heavy, sinking dread pressing on my chest. His eyes had opened, and in my heart, I believed we were finally stepping into recovery.

Each step toward the hospital felt lighter, more certain. I pictured him looking stronger — maybe even trying to move more.

Lakshay, Rohit bhaiya , and I entered the ICU together. As always, the guard uncle stood at the door. He never stopped the three of us from going in together, though he always limited others to one visitor at a time. Today, he smiled.

"He's moving his hands," he said.

The words went straight to my heart. Confidence swelled inside me, so much that, for the first time in days, I wanted to go first. Until now, I had always gone last — too afraid to see him like that.

But today, I stepped forward.

We had thirty minutes inside. I took the first twenty.

I stood by the left side of his bed — the side that still worked, while the right remained paralysed. His eyes were open, and when he looked at me, it felt almost normal again.

I could feel his pain — not just see it. We shared blood.

I held his left hand gently.

"Papa… are you okay?" I asked softly.

His fingers pressed against mine.

That was his answer.

I told him about the tube in his neck — how it was a sign of progress. The on-duty doctor had said physiotherapy had begun, three to four sessions a day, to keep his body moving. I explained everything to him, encouraging him to help in his own healing, to try harder so we could take him home sooner.

I checked the reports with Dr. Hemant on duty doctor in ICU ward. "Still critical," he said.

The word should have shaken me, but I looked at Papa's face — and saw hope. So I let the warning pass.

Hemant added that his blood pressure was under control now, and the CT scan showed no new bleeding or swelling.

I exhaled deeply. Relief filled me, spreading warmth through my chest.

Lakshay and I exchanged a glance — half laughter, half disbelief. For the first time, it felt like God had answered.

I told Rohit bhaiya to go home and rest, to focus on his work for a few days. We'd all been living in that hospital for too long.

I called Maa first, then Disha Didi — my voice bright with relief. For the first time, there was joy in our words.

In my heart, I was certain — nothing could happen to him now.

11 April — Early Morning

Around 4:00 a.m., Rohit bhaiya left for home. The drive was long, and he needed to return to work. He'd retired from the army but was now working in a school's management.

By 9:00 a.m., Lakshay and I were back at the hospital, as usual.

Papa had a mild fever, fluctuating between 100 and 102. But there was more movement than before. His reports were unchanged — stable, no new issues.

We communicated through signs.

If the answer was yes, he pressed our hand.

If no, he did nothing.

He understood everything.

We asked him simple, everyday questions to keep him engaged — to remind him he was still with us, still part of the world outside those machines. I could see the effort in his left hand, the slight tremor in his leg when he tried to move.

The ICU felt different that day — quieter. Peaceful, almost. For the first time, I wasn't panicking.

A Moment with Dr. Hemant

The nurse and Dr. Hemant, who often alternated shifts, came by. He smiled faintly and said,

"If I ever have a daughter, I'd want her to be like you. You haven't smiled for days, but you've done everything you could. You're half a doctor now. With how much you've learned about his condition, you could run a small clinic."

They laughed.

I laughed too — and took it as a compliment.

Afternoon with Dr. Ruhi

Later, Lakshay and I met Dr. Ruhi, as I did every day.

I always double-checked everything she said — then went home and googled each term. My engineering mind had turned obsessive; research had become my coping mechanism.

"How fast can he recover now?" I asked.

She didn't sugarcoat it.

"Recovery in such cases is very, very slow. You'll need patience. At least six to eight months before you'll see real progress."

I nodded.

Then I asked if I could return to work soon. She agreed.

So I decided — I'd work from here for the rest of the week, then head back to Bangalore next week.

For the first time in weeks, I made a plan that wasn't about fear — but about life moving forward.

CHAPTER 16

The Hope That Glimmered

12 April, 9:00 a.m.

We walked into the ICU the same way we had every day — but this morning felt different.

Papa's condition was better. Much better.

For the first time, I saw him lift his hand. His blood pressure was normal, his temperature steady. On the right side of his bed, a small box caught my eye.

I turned to Dr. Riya, the duty doctor.

"What's that?" I asked.

"It's sodium," she replied calmly.

As always, I leaned closer, scanning every reading, needing to know everything.

Every number, every beep could mean life or death.

She explained patiently, and only then did my restless mind ease.

Then came the real good news —

They had started reducing Papa's ventilator support. He was now breathing on his own for two hours, then back on support, then again without it — half and half.

For me, it was nothing short of a miracle.

Inside, my heart whispered — We're winning this battle.

I bent near him and whispered,

"Papa, are you okay? Do you need anything?"

Disha didi, handed me the wet wipes. She always said,

"Doctors don't bother with these small things. Keep his face clean."

She was right. Since his water went through the glucose pipe in his neck, his mouth stayed painfully dry. Sometimes he kept it open, struggling with the discomfort of the tracheostomy.

I gently wiped his lips, his face — like I had done from the first day.

Then I tested him like a child:

"Press my hand, Papa."

"Lift your leg."

"Open and close your eyes."

And he did — every single time. My heart could barely hold the joy.

But a thought gnawed at me.

In all these days, I had seen so many patients come and go — admitted in the ICU one week, shifted to the normal ward the next.

Why not Papa?

Why was he still here?

My patience was thinning, but his small signs of progress kept me holding on.

The April heat had begun to bite. Outside, summer was building — inside, we were planning.

Lakshay and I sat discussing.

"When Papa is discharged, how will we take him home? It's three hours away — too far, too risky."

So we decided — we wouldn't go home. We'd stay in the rented room nearby.

We'd make it comfortable for him — an AC, an air purifier (since his tracheostomy meant his lungs were exposed to even the smallest germ). We'd hire a nurse for the day. At night, Lakshay and I would take turns staying awake.

For the next six to eight months, we'd work from home — right there, by his side.

Even the house-owner uncle promised help.

I began enquiring about the AC, the purifier, the nurses — everything. My mind wouldn't rest until every arrangement was in place.

That afternoon, I met Dr. Ruhi.

Her words hit me like stones.

"Your father's TLC count is fluctuating," she said. "For a normal person, it should be around 11,000. His is between 13,000 and 18,000. It shows infection. The higher it goes, the more dangerous it becomes. It can reach his lungs, turn into pneumonia, even affect his heart."

I froze.

She added softly, "We're controlling it with antibiotics. But it depends on how his body reacts. Beyond that, we can only wait."

Her words echoed through me long after she left.

Papa wasn't weak — but he wasn't invincible either.

And then the calls began.

Relatives calling every day, telling their stories.

"Someone I know was worse — spent months in the hospital, and now he's fine, even driving again!"

Others said darkly, "Such patients never recover fully."

That's how Indian families are.

Some lift you up, others — knowingly or not — pull you down.

And you're left not knowing which words to hold on to.

13 April — Sunday

The hospital was quieter — no senior doctors, just the ICU staff moving softly through the corridors.

I told myself, I'll see Papa today and then finally book my ticket back to Bangalore. It's been too many days away from work. Life has to return to normal… right?

When I entered the ICU, my heart lifted.

Papa looked stronger — calmer, even. His vitals were steady. His eyes followed me when I walked closer.

For a moment, I felt he was silently telling me, Don't worry. I'm healing.

Relieved, I stepped outside and booked my ticket.

Chandigarh Airport. 18th April. 8:00 a.m.

As the confirmation message flashed on my phone, I didn't know whether to smile or cry.

My heart was split — one part clinging to his bedside, the other trying to drag me back to "normal life."

14 April

Mom was restless that morning.

My sister-in-law, Purvi, had to return to work — her flight was on the 15th. The thought of staying alone made Mom uneasy.

I asked her to come with us and see Papa's progress. She agreed.

At 9:00 a.m., during visiting hours, we entered the ICU together.

Mom stood beside Papa, watching him quietly, her eyes full of tears.

For those thirty minutes, Lakshay and I spoke to the doctors, checking every report. But I kept glancing at her.

There was relief on her face — pride, too. Pride that Papa was fighting through, pride that we had managed everything on time.

Later, she told us how proud she was.

She even cooked for us that day.

At lunch, we discussed the challenges ahead — how to manage once Papa was discharged. His one side was still paralyzed. We knew the care would demand constant effort.

I gently suggested that once he recovered a little, she should move with us to Bangalore so we could stay together.

But she refused — reminding me how she had lived alone when Papa was in the army. "I can manage again," she said.

I nodded, though inside, I worried for her.

That evening, Purvi joined us. Her flight was early next morning, so we all had dinner together.

The next day, after seeing Papa at 9:00 a.m., Mom also left for home. She was nervous, but I saw strength in her eyes.

She hugged me tightly before leaving. I booked her a cab, and my brother went along to drop her.

Later that day, I met Dr. Subham.

He gave me news that lit up my heart.

Papa was recovering — the blood clot was dissolving, the swelling had gone down, and he could lift his shoulder and make clear movements.

The ICU support was reduced — six hours without ventilation.

His TLC count had dropped to 12,000.

I couldn't believe it.

I looked up and whispered,

"Oh God, you truly exist. You saw our struggle. Thank you... I'll never forget this mercy."

17 April

That day, when Lakshay and I met Papa, I saw a version of him I had been praying for.

He could lift his shoulder, move his hand, even respond with clear signs. With support, he sat upright.

My heart swelled — overwhelmed, ecstatic, alive.

It felt like my soul was dancing just to see him like this.

But I needed clarity. Hope alone wasn't enough.

So at 2:00 p.m., I met Dr. Ruhi.

I asked her everything — his progress, his chances, his recovery, the timeline.

She answered gently, but truthfully.

"By next week, we'll likely shift him to the normal ward. But remember — now our part is over. The toughest part begins with you."

I frowned. "What do you mean?"

"One side of his body still doesn't work," she said. "He's a full-grown man. You'll need two to three people daily. At least one person must always be with him — for even his basic needs."

Her words made my stomach twist.

"How will we feed him?" I asked.

"Through the pipe," she replied. "We'll train you. You'll also need to learn suction — removing internal cough from his lungs and cleaning the tracheostomy pipe. Only when he starts generating cough on his own will we remove it. As the brain reconnects, the paralyzed side will slowly respond. It's possible — but it needs time, patience, and constant care."

I listened silently, my chest heavy.

Then I gathered myself and said, "Please arrange a nurse for at least two months. We'll pay whatever it takes. Also, tell me what kind of bed he'll need — because a normal one won't work."

She nodded. "We'll arrange both."

As I walked out, my mind was already racing. Feeding, cleaning, managing his every movement — it all waited ahead.

But giving up was not an option.

Right then, I decided —

I would take work from home for the next two to three months.

That's how we would manage.

No matter what it took.

CHAPTER 17
A Thousand Unsaid Words

I packed my bag slowly, each movement feeling impossibly heavy. My chest ached as though the last seventeen days had carved something permanent into me — an invisible scar that would never fade.

Those days had tested me beyond anything I'd ever known. I felt older now — sharper, burdened, carrying a weight I couldn't put down.

Lakshay slept peacefully in his room, untouched by the storm still raging inside me. I lay awake on the sofa, turning from one side to another, unable to still my mind. Thoughts looped endlessly — fear, hope, exhaustion — until they all blurred into one.

Papa would never be the same again.

He had always been the center of our world — the voice, the strength, the calm. And now, that anchor was fragile. He would need time, care, and vigilance. Life's chaos — once held together effortlessly by him — would now fall on us. We would have to become his shield, the same way he had always been ours.

Eighteen days had changed everything. Yet, beneath the exhaustion and fear, a small flame of gratitude flickered. God had heard us — He had given Papa back, even if not completely. I clung to that hope like it was air.

Sleep refused me. My mind kept spiraling — worry for Papa, concern for Lakshay, and the quiet terror of how fragile life had suddenly become.

By 4 a.m., I gave up trying to rest. I moved quietly, careful not to wake Lakshay, who for the first time in days slept soundly.

I busied myself with small things — washing his clothes, cleaning the kitchen, cooking breakfast — every motion an act of control against the chaos. I folded each shirt with precision, wiped every surface twice, as if order could protect us from what we couldn't control.

The room was still. Too still. Even the hum of the light felt loud, the tick of the clock sharp, every sound pressing against me like a warning I couldn't name.

For a moment, I paused and looked toward Lakshay's room. He slept deeply — finally, peacefully.

And yet, something inside me stirred uneasily.

I got ready quietly. My flight from Chandigarh was at 7:55 a.m. I planned to leave by 6:30 — the hospital was close, just five or six kilometers. The airport was small, check-in easy. It should've been a simple morning.

But my chest tightened as if the air itself resisted me. My body trembled, whispering what my mind refused to hear: Don't go.

I told myself it was just exhaustion — the residue of sleepless nights and hospital corridors — but the fear didn't ease.

I woke Lakshay. Together, we walked toward the hospital — my laptop bag slung across my shoulder, his hand gripping the trolley. The morning was still dark, air heavy and cool, the silence almost holy. Each step felt longer than the last, stretched by the weight of something I couldn't explain.

I kept talking — too much — spilling reminders and warnings in a desperate rush.

"Talk to the doctors every day. Double-check the reports. Don't trust them blindly. Keep the room clean so the owner lets us stay. Eat properly. Rest."

He nodded, quiet, obedient — half-awake, half-listening — but I couldn't stop. Each word felt like armor I was trying to leave behind.

When we reached the hospital gate, the world felt suspended. Only two guards stood there, silhouettes in the dull pre-dawn light. The street was silent, the air unmoving.

I asked to see Papa once more — just for a minute before leaving for Bangalore. They refused at first. Rules. Strict protocols.

I pleaded, my voice steady but urgent, threading desperation into calm words.

Finally, one of them relented.

"Okay… just for a minute."

Even as we walked through the gate, the air grew heavier. My heartbeat was loud in my ears. Each step toward the ICU pulled at my chest, as if some invisible thread was trying to hold me back.

I pushed open the ICU door, half-running inside — part fear, part instinct.

"Papa!"

My voice cut through the hum of machines.

He was resting — but the instant he heard me, his eyes shot open.

Wide. Alert. Searching.

For a second, everything else disappeared — the monitors, the quiet nurses, the sleeping patients. The world narrowed to his eyes and mine.

The nurse noticed and rushed over.

"You're not allowed in at this time," she said firmly.

"I'm leaving for Bangalore," I whispered. "Please. I just need to see him once."

A long pause. Then, a nod.

I stepped closer. The familiar table stood beside his bed — the same one where doctors had handed me forms, reports, impossible words. But today, it felt different. Final. Heavy.

Papa's gaze locked onto mine. His eyes were restless, full of questions I couldn't answer.

Why are you dressed? Where are you going?

I spoke softly, forcing steadiness into my trembling voice.

"Papa… you're doing so well. The doctors said you'll be shifted to the normal ward soon. Lakshay will stay here with you. And Maa's alone at home — I need to be with her."

He lifted his left hand. I took it gently.

"If it's okay… press my hand."

He pressed. Hard. Too hard.

It wasn't just a gesture — it was a cry. His eyes filled with a desperate intensity, as if he was trying to tell me something urgent, something beyond words. The tracheostomy blocked his voice, but his hand spoke volumes.

He pressed again. And again.

Each squeeze a pulse of fear, love, something I couldn't name — something that burned straight through me.

The nurse came back, urging me to leave. But I couldn't. My fingers wouldn't let go.

Time blurred. I lingered, memorizing his face, his eyes, the feel of his palm against mine.

Finally, I whispered, "Papa… I have to go."

I tried to pull away, but he reached out again — fingertips brushing mine, clinging, trembling.

I waved goodbye; he waved me back — once, twice, again — as if refusing to let me go. His eyes were wide and wet, full of words his mouth couldn't form.

I stepped out of the ICU with my heart crushed between beats. The air outside was thick, unmoving. The city was silent. Even the light felt dimmer.

Each step toward the auto felt like a goodbye I wasn't ready to say.

Even on the flight to Bangalore, I could still feel the echo of his gaze — that silent press of his hand — and the unspoken words that would follow me for the rest of my life.

CHAPTER 18

When Life Hangs by a Thread

When I reached Bangalore, it was the weekend. I tried to slip back into my old routine, but it felt like stepping into a world I no longer knew. The last few weeks had been so heavy, so suffocating, that I had forgotten how to live a normal day.

I forced myself into practical tasks — house hunting, errands, decisions that once felt trivial. By Sunday, I finalized a small, modest apartment. Deliberately cheap. Papa was still in the hospital, and once he was discharged, I would return to him. Why waste money on a locked flat?

But life has a way of testing certain people harder than others. And I am one of them. It pushes you into fire, deeper than you think you can survive, and just when you believe you've endured enough, it lands another blow.

My professional life had been my refuge — my one constant, my strongest ground. I had worked relentlessly, immersing myself in tasks until nothing else existed. That belief, that work alone defined life, was my biggest mistake.

When I returned to the office after weeks of trauma, I hoped for at least some stability there. But the shadows followed me.

A meeting with my manager felt like a wall collapsing on me. Her words were calm, calculated, merciless.

"You've been absent for eighteen days," she said. "We're not happy. We'll have to roll you off."

Eighteen days. Eighteen days when my father's life hung by a thread. Eighteen days I chose to save his breath over meeting deadlines. Did she even care? No. She had already decided.

I had followed every rule — applied for leave without pay — yet corporate walls bend for profit, not humanity. Empathy was weakness. Compassion was a liability.

Her decision was final. She didn't want to hear my side. My soul, already bruised, felt a fresh sting. Corporate life can be crueler than any political battlefield. In glass towers, your fall is decided in seconds, without hesitation, without mercy.

I swallowed it. I had no fight left. Pain had numbed me; experience had taught me that masks walked on legs, pretending to care, waiting for the moment to strike.

It was 23rd April. That morning, I decided I wouldn't go to the office. I would work from home, however little I could manage.

Then the phone rang.

It was Lakshay. His voice trembled, breaking.

"Lakshay, how is Papa?" I asked.

He paused. "…Today?"

"What? Tell me!"

"Papa's TLC count… 19,000. Dangerous. Fever. He hasn't opened his eyes since last night."

Fear stabbed my chest. My voice shook.

"No… no! We can't wait. We must shift him today — at any cost."

Lakshay's voice was strained. "The doctor… he's very critical."

Frantic calls followed. Every contact, every thread of hope became a lifeline. Finally, through army connections, we arranged support to shift Papa to Nest Hospital — just five minutes away, yet it felt like another universe.

Lakshay handled the discharge papers, medical summaries, reports. I hovered, restless, unable to trust that anything would go smoothly. After days of watching, questioning, monitoring every update, this sudden collapse felt like betrayal. Survival was the only focus.

The process crawled like a nightmare. Hospitals know how to stretch every second when urgency is life itself. Even in critical condition, they insisted on changing his hospital attire — as if the uniform mattered more than his life. I pleaded, but Lakshay was tense, too exhausted to argue. Every delay cut into me.

Finally, the ambulance arrived. By 7 p.m., Papa was moving. My chest, taut for hours, loosened only when Lakshay confirmed he had reached the ICU of the new hospital.

By 10 p.m., he was inside, under strict, competent care. Lakshay , exhausted and starving, had barely eaten. Yet through his voice came relief. "This place is different," he said. Clean. Professional. Disciplined. Strict rules, controlled ICU visits. It gave him comfort — and through him, me too.

Regret hit me hard. Why hadn't we shifted him sooner? But I whispered a prayer of gratitude. At last, Papa was in a place where healing felt possible.

CHAPTER 19

The Dream That Felt Real

I called Lakshay the next morning. His voice was calmer this time, steadier. He told me he was still at the hospital. Unlike the previous one, this place felt… humane. There was enough space for attendants to rest, to breathe. He had even carried his laptop along, determined to work from there — to be near Papa, to keep watch every single moment.

Hearing that brought a strange relief. At least someone I trusted was standing guard.

The man who had made this shift possible — our lifeline in that desperate hour — was Dinesh's friend. Dinesh, my brother-in-law, whom I always called Jiju out of respect. The word itself carried a quiet dignity, a bridge of trust.

That day, I heard Jiju was coming to the hospital himself — to see Papa, to see his condition with his own eyes. Somehow, that knowledge soothed me. For once, it didn't feel like we were fighting this battle alone.

Later that morning, Jiju called. His voice carried a new firmness.

"This hospital is different," he said. "They have people here — powerful ones — who'll make sure your father gets every possible help."

Then he told me something that made my stomach twist. Papa had finally been given a rare, costly injection — one meant for brain hemorrhage patients in the earliest hours. A life-saving shot… if given in time. But the previous hospital had never administered it. Whether they didn't have it, didn't know, or simply didn't care — I'll never know.

My throat went dry. I could only clutch the bedsheet and whisper, "Okay."

Jiju promised he would reach by 2 or 3 p.m., see Papa himself, and then update me. That fragile assurance became the only rope I could hold on to.

I tried to work. Tried to bury myself in my laptop. But my fingers moved on their own while my mind stayed locked inside the ICU. My body was in my room, yet my soul hovered over Papa's bed — restless, sleepless, circling. I hadn't truly slept in days. My heart ached with a kind of exhaustion that no words could carry.

Finally, I told myself, just a few minutes… just close your eyes.

But what came wasn't rest.

It was something else.

I don't even remember falling asleep. All I know is that suddenly — Papa was there.

Standing. Whole. Alive. Smiling.

He wasn't the fragile man I'd last seen on that hospital bed. He was himself again — strong, radiant. He wore his favorite outfit: a grey-white kurta-pajama, a soft peach sweater, his dark brown jacket, and his Himachali cap perched perfectly on his head. His teeth flashed in that familiar, full smile. His eyes twinkled. His hands hung straight at his sides, steady, confident.

It wasn't a dream. Dreams are hazy, blurred.

This was crystal clear. Every detail — the color of his sweater, the tilt of his cap, the warmth in his eyes — it was all real.

For a moment, the hospital machines, the panic, the suffering — everything dissolved. All that existed was him. Papa. Whole again.

Then I jolted awake. My heart thundered in my chest, loud and painful. The room was empty. Silent. Still.

It wasn't just a dream.

It was a message.

A signal from God.

Tears blurred my vision as I whispered to myself, "He's coming back. He'll recover."

I grabbed my phone and called Lakshay, my voice trembling as I told him everything. He listened quietly, then said, "You know what… I feel it too. I can't explain it, but I know he's going to be fine."

I clung to that sentence like oxygen — He's going to be fine.

When I asked about Papa, Lakshay said visitors weren't allowed yet. The doctors needed time. "Don't disturb them," he told me gently. "These people know what they're doing. Trust them."

For the first time in days, I tried to still my restless heart. Let them do their work, I told myself.

By then, Jiju had reached the hospital. When I spoke to him, his words steadied me again. "I'll stay till evening," he said firmly. "I'll only leave once I've looked into the doctors' eyes and heard it myself."

I wanted to believe him. I wanted to believe everything was finally turning around. That the worst was over.

For the first time in days, I let myself breathe.

But deep inside, hidden beneath that fragile hope, a shadow stirred — quiet and cold.

Because sometimes, dreams that feel too real aren't promises of tomorrow.

Finger crossed!!!

CHAPTER 20

The Night I Lost My Voice to Prayer

It was around 6 p.m. when I called Lakshay again to ask about Papa's condition.

The moment he spoke, something inside me broke—his voice trembled, fragile, defeated.

"Papa is not well," he said quietly. "He's not opening his eyes."

The world tilted. My chest caved in. I could hear my heartbeat slamming inside my skull.

That was it—the moment when air stopped feeling like air.

The moment I knew something was terribly, irreversibly wrong.

I called Jiju in panic. His tone was calm—too calm, like someone trying to cover an open wound.

"Every hospital has its own process," he said evenly. "You have to be patient. Since things were delayed, it will take some time to stabilize."

I nodded, but my insides screamed.

How do you ask a daughter to be patient when her father's eyes won't open?

Minutes crawled like hours.

Then Lakshay called again—his whisper slicing through my chest:

"Start reading Hanuman Chalisa."

That sentence… it shattered me.

We only say Hanuman Chalisa when the impossible closes in, when science stops and only miracles remain.

With shaking hands, I opened the app on my phone and began chanting. My voice cracked between words. Every verse felt like a thread tying me to Papa's soul, as if my prayers could pull him back from wherever he was drifting.

After each round, I called again—begging for a heartbeat of hope.

Then Lakshay's voice returned, thinner, fading.

"This time… it's different," he said. "He's critical. The doctors are giving him CPR."

"Whaaat?" My voice tore apart.

CPR? I didn't even understand what that meant. Was it an injection? A treatment?

"Google it," he whispered.

I did.

And what I saw destroyed me—images of doctors pressing against lifeless chests, machines beeping frantically, faces frozen in desperation.

My hands went numb. My body turned to ice. My heart rattled inside me like a trapped bird.

Please, God. Please.

If I've ever done anything right, pay me back today.

Not him. Not now.

Jiju repeated the same thing Lakshay had said. "They've given CPR. They said he might survive. But we have to wait… two hours."

Two hours.

How do you measure eternity in hours?

I picked up my phone again and chanted louder, faster—like if I could outrun death, Papa would wake up.

I bargained with God, hysterically.

Take everything. My prayers. My dreams. My years ahead.

But not him. Please, not him.

The phone would ring, then go silent.

Each silence screamed louder than words.

"Why isn't Lakshay picking up?" I asked Jiju.

"He's sitting in the hospital temple," Jiju whispered. "He hasn't stopped praying."

When Lakshay finally answered, his voice was barely there.

"Don't stop," he begged. "Keep chanting. Not even for a second."

By then my lips were raw. My throat burned. But I didn't stop. I promised myself I'd reach a thousand chants. Maybe then, maybe God would have to listen.

By 10:30 p.m., I called Mummy. My voice shook as I told her Papa was critical.

"Light a diya in the temple," I pleaded.

She was already crying, her voice trembling as she said she would.

Moments later, my phone rang again—Jiju.

My chest tightened. I answered, breathless.

"He's fine now, right?" I asked. "It's been two hours… he's okay, isn't he?"

The pause on the other end sliced through me.

"No," Jiju said softly. "He's still very critical. The doctors say if he sees all his children… maybe he'll recover faster. You should book your ticket and come immediately."

My world shattered.

"Come?" I screamed. "What do you mean come? Has something happened? Why are you hiding things from me? Why isn't anyone saying it clearly?"

"He's with the doctors," Jiju murmured. "Just… take the first flight and come."

I hung up and called Mummy again, trembling. "Why are they asking me to come?"

Her silence said everything she didn't.

I couldn't tell her what I feared. I couldn't destroy her with the truth I was still running from.

I opened my laptop with shaking hands. The screen blurred through my tears. I searched for flights blindly. Found one—4 a.m.—and booked it without thinking.

Then another call came.

Disha didi My sister. From Mummy's phone.

Her voice was swollen from crying, though she tried to sound steady.

"Did you book the flight?" she asked.

"Yes," I said. "For 4 a.m."

"Why not earlier?" she pressed, voice cracking.

"There was no urgent one," I whispered. "But why are you calling from Mummy's phone?"

Silence. Then:

"I've reached home," she said.

My head spun. Home? Why? What did that mean?

Something wasn't right. Something was being kept from me.

But I clung to denial.

If it was truly over, they'd be screaming, wailing. The world would've already ended.

No—he was just serious. He was fighting. He'd open his eyes when we all reached.

I lied to myself just to breathe.

I dragged out my trolley bag, throwing clothes in—unmatched, unfolded, I didn't care. Laptop, charger, slippers. My hands were moving, but my mind was somewhere far away.

I locked the door, though my heart was already open and bleeding.

As I stepped out, the phone rang again. Disha didi

Her voice was heavier this time, like every syllable cost her pain.

"Do one thing," she said softly. "Get Purvi also. I've called her. She's getting ready. Book her ticket too."

I froze. My breath hitched.

"Why Purvi? Why now?" I asked, my voice cracking. "Why do you need both of us to come together? Is everything okay?"

A silence. Then a forced answer:

"Yes… yes, everything's fine. Just bring her too."

But my heart knew what her words were hiding.

One part of me screamed, No!

God cannot do this. Not to me. Not after everything.

He's seen my faith—He wouldn't betray it.

But the quieter voice inside me—the one that always knew before the truth arrived—whispered what I couldn't bear to hear:

If Papa is only critical, why are they calling everyone home?

Still, I clung to hope like a wounded child.

Maybe he's waiting for us. Maybe he'll open his eyes when he hears our voices.

Maybe… maybe.

But somewhere deep within me, the ground had already begun to crack.

CHAPTER 21
The Aura That Carried Me

I was trapped inside my own thoughts, drowning in fear, replaying the same questions until they clawed at my skull.

What had happened? Why had they called so suddenly? Why Purvi too? Why now?

Was it a tragedy? Was something already over—and they were calling me for what?

My chest tightened. My breath refused to flow.

I forced myself into an auto, too afraid to take a private cab—terrified that if I was alone and panic struck, I wouldn't survive it. My mind was already a battlefield. But when I reached the bus stand, what I saw was worse than anything inside my head.

The place was dead.

It was almost 11 p.m. The market that usually hummed with rickshaws, vendors, and tired footsteps was swallowed by a silence so thick it pressed against my skin.

No buses. No autos. No cars. No voices. Not even a stray dog prowling the shadows.

The air felt hollow, as if the city had exhaled once—and never inhaled again.

I froze.

My skin prickled.

My heart refused to accept it.

How could this place be so empty?

How could silence be this loud?

Each step I took felt wrong, too sharp, too loud against the stillness. My ears strained for sound, any sound—but there was nothing. It didn't feel like night. It felt like the world itself had stopped breathing.

I clutched my phone with trembling hands and booked an Uber.

Fifteen minutes.

Just fifteen.

But those fifteen minutes stretched before me like an endless corridor of fear.

My legs no longer belonged to me.

They were heavy, numb—dragging against the earth as if gravity itself was grieving.

My body felt like ice wrapped in skin, my brain spinning like a wheel without a center, my heart hammering so violently I thought it might break free from my ribs.

Dragging my trolley bag behind me, laptop biting into my shoulder, I realized I didn't even have the strength to lift something as light as a needle.

And for the first time that night, I couldn't call anyone.

Not Lakshay Not Disha didi Not Jiju. Not even Mummy.

My fingers ached to dial, but my soul refused.

Because one word—just one—could end me.

I didn't want to know. I wasn't ready.

Because knowing meant accepting.

And I was not ready—not one percent.

This could not be his time.

God couldn't do this. Not now. Not ever.

If He took my father, I would lose faith forever.

My father—the man who gave without asking, who stood between me and every storm, who never demanded but always gave—he wasn't just my father. He was my safety. My provider. My anchor in a ruthless world.

The only person who expected nothing, yet gave everything.

How does a body keep living if God steals away the soul that sustains it?

Who would dare touch my father's breath?

Who has that right?

He couldn't go.

He wouldn't go.

Clutching my chest, I prayed, words breaking into jagged whispers, my throat tightening until sound barely escaped.

God, I trust You with all that I am. You know my heart is not ready. Don't take him. Please. Not him.

As I stood there—lost inside that storm of denial and terror—the headlights appeared in the distance: two faint eyes piercing through the dark, drawing closer.

The cab moved through the empty streets, headlights slicing the night, but my mind wasn't inside that car anymore.

It was running wild, chasing questions that had no answers.

What must have happened? Why was I called? Why Purvi too? Was it already over?

My chest burned. My throat closed. The air itself felt like betrayal.

And then—something shifted.

It was sudden, like the air cracked open.

One heartbeat I was drowning in panic.

The next, I froze.

Because something entered.

Not through the door. Not through the window.

Through me.

The space filled—charged, heavy, yet comforting. The kind of weight you don't fight. The kind that pins you down but makes you feel safe.

And I knew instantly. I didn't need proof. I didn't need words.

My soul recognized it before my mind could.

It was him.

My father.

Not in flesh, not in sound—but in presence.

The cab seemed to dissolve around me. The driver's movements slowed, unreal, as if time itself bowed.

The city had no pulse, no sound. Everything stopped breathing—except me, and him.

And in that moment, my fear fractured.

The panic that had ruled me for hours shattered like glass, and in its place came something else—light.

Not the kind you see. The kind you feel.

It wrapped around me, pressing against my skin, sliding into my chest, flooding me with warmth that both burned and soothed.

Love.

Pure, unbearable love—the kind that breaks you because it's too much for one heart to hold.

Tears spilled without warning. My lips trembled, but no sound came. Because I understood.

This wasn't a visit.

It was a farewell.

He hadn't come to stay.

He had come to let me know—he was leaving.

A goodbye dressed as comfort.

I wanted to scream, to beg, to stop time. But all I could do was sit there, frozen, while his presence poured through me like a tide. He was pulling something out of me—my terror, my grief, my denial—taking it with him, so I wouldn't be crushed beneath its weight.

The world faded. The road vanished. I wasn't in a car anymore.

I was nowhere. And everywhere.

And in that timeless nowhere—I felt him.

The same strength that once held my hand.

The same protection that once stood between me and storms.

The same love that never asked, never demanded—only gave.

He didn't need words. The silence spoke.

I am here. I will always be here. But this is goodbye.

My chest cracked open. My tears were no longer from fear—they were from knowing.

And then, slowly, he began to fade.

The warmth slipping. The light receding. The air growing cold again.

The tide went back.

And I was left on the shore—raw, trembling, reaching for the emptiness he left behind.

The cab came back into focus.

The sound of tires. The glow of streetlights. Time had returned.

But I wasn't the same.

Because I knew—with a certainty sharper than any blade—my father's soul had come to me, one last time, only to say goodbye.

***

The cab stopped. I was at the airport.

And that's when I felt it—the shift.

The warmth that had carried me through the dark was suddenly gone. Just… gone.

It was like being thrown back into my body after floating beyond it.

I was no longer light. I was heavy. Shaking. Broken. Drowning in grief that clawed its way back into my chest.

Tears burned my eyes. My throat ached. My heart thrashed like it wanted out.

That eternity when love had held me—was over.

And I hated it.

I wanted it back.

I wanted him back.

I dragged my luggage through the glass doors of the terminal.

My sister-in-law was already there, waiting.

We didn't speak much.

What words exist for this kind of waiting? For this kind of fear?

The clock crawled.

My flight was at 4 a.m., but every passing minute was punishment.

The chairs were cold. The lights too bright. The world indifferent.

How could life move when mine had stopped?

I sat beside her, trembling, my mind a pendulum swinging between prayer and dread.

The silence between us was heavy, filled with all the questions we didn't dare ask.

And beneath it all, one truth kept whispering—

the aura that had carried me here was gone.

Maybe it came only to keep me steady.

Maybe it was… a final gift.

He can't be gone, I told myself. He just can't.

Because no one had said those words.

Because Lakshay hadn't told me.

Because Jiju hadn't said it.

Because if such a storm had struck, I would have been the first to know.

They told me something else—that he wasn't well, but maybe, maybe if he saw us, things could turn.

So I clung to that maybe.

Built my breath around it.

Repeated it like a mantra: He is waiting for me. He has to be.

But even as I whispered it, another voice rose inside me—the one that remembered the aura, the warmth, the fading light.

What if that wasn't comfort?

What if it was goodbye?

The thought sliced through me. I tried to bury it, but it kept rising, like a ghost that refused to leave.

Beside me, my sister-in-law sat with folded hands, eyes red, facc pale.

We didn't speak.

Because words, right now, were grenades—one wrong syllable and everything would explode.

The flight was at 4 a.m.

2:10. 2:45. 3:05.

Every number on the display felt like a hammer inside my skull.

I leaned back, fingers gripping the chair's edge.

Closed my eyes.

And then—memories.

They came like shards of glass. I pressed my palms to my face, but they cut through anyway.

A sob tore out of me. My body folded in half, forehead against my knees.

My sister-in-law touched my back, gently—but even that couldn't reach the storm inside.

Around us, the airport buzzed with life.

People boarding, wheels rolling, announcements echoing.

The world kept moving.

By 3:45, when boarding began, my body felt decades older.

Each step toward the gate was a prayer and a punishment.

He's waiting for me. He'll open his eyes when I arrive, I whispered.

But deep down, I knew.

That aura—the warmth, the silence, the goodbye—

was already the answer I was too afraid to hear.

And between those two voices, I walked into the night—broken, trembling, clinging to the fragile belief that maybe, just maybe, I was not too late.

CHAPTER 22

The Weight of That Moment

The plane took off, its roar filling my chest, and for the next three hours, I was a prisoner inside my own skin.

I couldn't close my eyes. Not even for a second. Every time my eyelids dared to fall, terror jolted me awake—because what if sleep meant surrender? What if closing my eyes meant losing the last fragile thread keeping him alive inside me?

I sat rigid in my narrow seat, fingers gripping the armrest until my nails carved half-moons into the plastic. The hum of the engine was too steady, too alive, mocking me with a heartbeat that wasn't his.

Around me, strangers slept—peaceful, weightless, unaware that for someone among them, the world was ending at thirty thousand feet.

My mind raced in endless circles, crashing into itself:

Is he still breathing? What if I'm too late? What if that warmth I felt wasn't hope—but farewell?

Time stretched cruelly. Minutes didn't pass—they bled.

I tried to pray, but even my prayers trembled. My lips moved, but inside, only one word thundered again and again, like a drum I couldn't silence—

Don't. Don't. Don't.

I refused to blink for too long, as if my vigilance could rewrite fate. Maybe if I stayed awake—if I suffered enough—God would notice and trade my pain for mercy.

And so, for three endless hours, I stayed awake in that dark cabin, trapped between earth and sky, carrying a fear so heavy it became the only luggage I couldn't put down.

The plane finally shuddered against the runway. People exhaled, seatbelts clicked open, voices rose—carefree, relieved.

But not me.

My nightmare wasn't the flight. It was what waited on the ground.

The flight attendant's voice came faintly:

"You may now switch on your phones."

My hand froze.

I couldn't.

Because the moment I pressed that button, the truth would hit like lightning.

What if one message—one sentence—ended my world?

I stared at the black screen as if it were a loaded gun.

Around me, screens lit up, notifications chimed, laughter stirred.

But mine stayed dark. Dead. Silent.

Don't do it, my mind whispered. Just one more minute. One more minute where hope still lives.

But hope is cruel.

It makes you press the button anyway.

The screen flared bright.

My heart nearly cracked from the sound of silence that followed.

No messages.

No missed calls.

Nothing.

I blinked, disbelief flooding me. If something had happened—if the unthinkable had really torn through my life—my phone would have been burning in my hands.

But it was still. Quiet.

And for a fleeting second, I let myself believe—

Maybe he's still here. Maybe he's waiting.

My hands shook as I dialed Lakshay

Once. Twice. Again.

No answer.

Each ring sliced deeper, until it wasn't sound anymore—it was pain.

I scrolled and found Jiju's number.

He picked up immediately.

"Where are you?" His voice was thick, uneven.

"At the airport," I whispered. "Tell me, Jiju, how is Papa? Which hospital? I'll go straight there."

Silence.

Long. Too long.

The kind of silence that doesn't hide truth—it delivers it.

Then softly, he said,

"Beta… just come home directly."

My whole body locked.

"What? NO!" The scream ripped from me, sharp, animal. "Why home? You said he was critical. Then he's in the hospital, right? RIGHT? I'll go there! He's waiting for me—he has to be!"

My words spilled wild, frantic, like I could force reality to bend through sheer refusal.

"Beta..." Jiju's voice broke. "Doctors said... he has very little time left. They asked us to give him love... and care... at home."

The phone trembled in my hand.

At home.

Not hospital.

At home.

The words echoed like knives against bone. My lips moved—No. No. No.—but my heart already knew.

I knew what he hadn't said.

Papa was gone.

That warmth I'd felt, that unbearable comfort in the cab—it hadn't been hope. It had been his soul's last embrace. His final goodbye.

And now, all I had left was the cruel silence of the living.

I opened the cab app. The letters blurred behind tears. My chest split in two—

Brain screaming one truth.

Heart begging another.

Brain: He's gone. If there was even a flicker of life, he'd still be inside the ICU, breathing through machines. You know this.

Heart: No one said the word gone. Until someone says it aloud, he's alive. He must be.

I booked the cab.

Every second waiting was a noose tightening around my throat.

Around me—laughter, footsteps, families reuniting.

The world kept moving.

How could it?

I stepped outside. The air slapped me cold. My body walked, but my mind stayed behind—in denial, in prayer, in a time that had already ended.

Headlights flashed.

The cab stopped.

I climbed in.

And inside that moving box of silence—I broke. Not into two, not ten—but into a thousand jagged pieces.

Every turn of the wheels dragged me closer to truth.

To home.

To him.

Or what was left of him.

When the car stopped, I saw the crowd before I saw the door.

Neighbors. Relatives. Strangers.

Faces I barely recognized—all standing still, all silent.

Their silence screamed.

I stepped into the courtyard—and I knew.

I didn't need words.

The air itself told me.

Heavy. Still. Soaked in sorrow.

The kind of air that only exists when a house has lost its heart.

And then—I saw him.

My Papa.

Still. Silent. Draped in white.

The sight tore something open in me that will never close again.

My knees buckled. My scream didn't sound human.

It was the sound of a soul being ripped from itself.

"PAPA!"

I fell forward, clawing the earth, begging, shaking. My body convulsed with grief so violent it felt like it could kill me.

Hands tried to hold me—Jiju, Maasi, neighbors—but I tore away.

I didn't want comfort.

I wanted him.

I stumbled inside. Every step was a wound.

And when I reached him, I collapsed beside his still body, clutching his chest, sobbing into the white cloth that separated me from everything I loved.

"Papa… please wake up. I came. I'm here. Please don't leave me. Please…"

But he didn't move.

He had already slipped into the silence of forever.

The world spun.

I wept until breathing hurt. Until the room disappeared.

Until there was nothing left—only me and him.

Me alive.

Him gone.

And no amount of tears could reach where he had gone.

CHAPTER 23
The Silence That Stays

It has been exactly four months since he left.

24 April — the day he left us. 24 August — the day I finished writing this book.

Four months, and yet the wound has never closed.

Grief does not see you as human.

It does not care for hours, or sleep, or breath.

It bleeds you slowly—day after day, night after night—until the edges of your soul begin to fray.

I am left with a storm inside me—heartbreak that shreds, regrets that burn.

All the things I could have done differently, all the moments I could have held him tighter… maybe, just maybe, I could have saved him.

But I couldn't.

And now I carry that weight—sharp, endless, and alive.

We don't grow. We age.

Experience teaches the world to move forward, but it never teaches you how to survive losing the one who made you feel alive.

I don't know what he felt in those final moments.

I don't know what he thought.

All I know is that life has left me hollow—breathing, yet lifeless.

I cannot care for anything anymore.

Books, music, laughter, the sun—nothing touches me now.

I tell myself that time will make it bearable, that someday I'll learn to accept it.

But not today.

Not this hour.

Not this second.

Because right now, my soul screams so loud I can almost hear it tearing itself apart.

No sound leaves my mouth—it's deeper than that.

It's a cry born in the bones, echoing from the place where love once lived.

To forget him? Impossible.

He lives in my blood, in my marrow, in every breath I take.

He made me. Guided me. Trusted me. Loved me.

How do I repay that?

How do I honor the sacrifices he made?

I can't.

I don't even know where to begin.

Everywhere I look—his clothes folded neatly, his diaries lying silent, his slippers by the door, the room that still smells like him—

they stab me.

A thousand knives. A thousand flames.

A thousand thousand shards tearing through my chest.

Every memory, a blade.

Every breath, a betrayal.

And I am left here—shattered.

A body moving through space, but a soul ripped to pieces.

Screaming, silently, in a world that has no mercy.

I read a quote... and it did not just touch me — it tore something inside me.

It made my soul cry. Not softly. Not silently. But loud... unbearably loud.

As if someone had taken a sharp memory and pressed it hard against my living heart.

The quote said:

"Few years back you signed my birth certificate, and today I signed your death certificate."

And in that single line, my entire world collapsed again.

How cruel is time...

The same hands that once celebrated my arrival in this world...

The same name that wrote my beginning...

One day, I had to write his ending.

A father signs his child's birth with hope, with dreams, with trembling happiness.

But a child signing a father's death…

That signature is not ink.

It is grief.

It is shock.

It is a wound that never truly closes.

When I read it, I did not just understand it — I lived it.

Every word felt like it knew my story.

Like it had seen me standing there… holding the pen… while my heart refused to accept what my hand was doing.

Some truths don't scream outside.

They scream within.

And today, that quote made my soul scream.

Your loose is permanent my dear father. No one can replace you ever . Love you papa 🖤🖤🖤